Journal of Media and Religion
Volume 2, Number 1, 2003

Special Issue:
Framing Religion in the News

T0347927

Journal Information

Subscriptions: *Journal of Media and Religion* is published quarterly by Lawrence Erlbaum Associates, Inc., 10 Industrial Avenue, Mahwah, NJ 07430–2262. Subscriptions for Volume 2, 2003, are available only on a calendar-year basis.

Individual rates: **Print *Plus* Online:** $40.00 in USA, $70.00 outside USA. Institutional rates: **Print-Only:** $160.00 in USA, $190.00 outside USA. **Online-Only:** $160.00 in USA and outside USA. **Print *Plus* Online:** $180.00 in USA, $210.00 outside USA. Visit LEA's Web site at http://www.erlbaum.com to view a free sample.

Order subscriptions through the Journal Subscription Department, Lawrence Erlbaum Associates, Inc., 10 Industrial Avenue, Mahwah, NJ 07430–2262.

Claims: Claims for missing copies cannot be honored beyond 4 months after mailing date. Duplicate copies cannot be sent to replace issues not delivered due to failure to notify publisher of change of address.

Change of Address: Send address changes to the Journal Subscription Department, Lawrence Erlbaum Associates, Inc., 10 Industrial Avenue, Mahwah, NJ 07430–2262.

Permissions: Requests for permission should be sent to the Permissions Department, Lawrence Erlbaum Associates, Inc., 10 Industrial Avenue, Mahwah, NJ 07430–2262.

Abstracts/Indexes: This journal is abstracted or indexed in *EBSCOhost Products; ComIndex; ComAbstracts; Communications Abstracts;* and *Linguistics and Language Behavior Abstracts.*

Microform Copies: Microform copies of this journal are available through ProQuest Information and Learning, P.O. Box 1346, Ann Arbor, MI 48106–1346. For more information, call 1–800–521–0600, ext. 2888.

Copyright © 2003, Lawrence Erlbaum Associates, Inc. No part of this publication may be used, in any form or by any means, without permission of the publisher.

Visit LEA's Web site at **http://www.erlbaum.com**

ISSN 1534–8423

JOURNAL OF MEDIA AND RELIGION, 2(1), 1–3

EDITORS' INTRODUCTION

Media, Religion, and "Framing"

Daniel A. Stout

Department of Communications
Brigham Young University

Judith M. Buddenbaum

Department of Journalism and Technical Communication
Colorado State University

How religion is depicted by journalists is a key area of interest to researchers of media and religion. Scholars sharply disagree in their interpretations of news coverage. Olasky (1990) claimed that the press has been secularized in its framing of religion, whereas Silk (1995) insisted that religious values are clearly reflected in this type of news. Despite their tendency to dichotomize the issue, Olasky and Silk focus us on an important question: What is the nature of the process by which journalists present religion to their audiences? One approach to this issue, which has not been adequately applied to the study of media and religion, is *framing*.

At the most basic level, *frame analysis* (Goffman, 1974) is the study of how events in everyday life are organized or made sense of in coherent ways. We react to things in the world based on the information coming to us through frames. Mass media frame events by organizing them into news stories, which are the products of a journalist's perceptions and a business organization's effort to attract audiences.

In the study of religion and media, framing has value far beyond just knowing what is in the news; it also determines the types of information that ultimately contribute to public opinion about particular religions. Knowing what type of information is out there is very important given that treatment of religious groups is tied to the kinds of information available to citizens. Support-oriented frames by the

---

Requests for reprints should be sent to Daniel A. Stout, E-509 HFAC, Brigham Young University, Provo, UT 84602–1422. E-mail: daniel_stout@byu.edu

Gilded Age press of Chicago helped facilitate revivalism and religious fervor in the late 19th century (Evensen, 2000). However, in Nazi Germany, newspapers framed stories in ways that ostracized Jews and invited persecution (Lasswell, 1971). It is often indirect, but inevitably, there is some relation between media framing and social processes such as religious assimilation and accommodation.

Framing of religion news has changed dramatically throughout U.S. history. In the early American colonial period, much printed news was religious news. In an era characterized as a "religious haven" (Williams, 2000, p. 2), printed material reflected the views of Quakers, Catholics, Huguenots, and other groups in the late 1600s. Puritan theology also had a strong influence on the content of early newspapers (Sloan, 2000).

Although the history of the American press is one of diverse editorial perspectives and content, prior to 1900, there were periods of great sensitivity to the religious worldview in America's periodicals. By the 1830s, however, the concept of "religion news" was established (Buddenbaum, 1998). That is, religion was no longer dominant, but was presented alongside other news items related to agriculture, business, and culture.

Most of the 20th century was characterized by a distinction between religious and secular media. The mainstream press evolved in a secular direction as citizens and lawmakers demanded greater separation of church and state. Economic interests and the desire to attract advertisers also reduced religion's prominence in the daily press with many papers relegating it to the weekly religion page. Buddenbaum (1998) concluded that these developments "now make religious journalism of the kind practiced openly by earlier generations the province of specialized publications" (p. 92).

Recent developments have ushered in a new era of religion news where framing analysis is particularly relevant and useful. The emerging "information society" is creating unique challenges for religious institutions and the journalists who cover them (Schement & Stephenson, 1996). One such challenge is the transition by religious groups from private sphere to public sphere. New media have increased the number of situations in which the actions of religious individuals are often made public, and more people are brought into the public discussion. Meyrowitz (1994) summarized this trend in terms of a loss of physical place due to the mediated environment of information technology. How will journalists frame religion in this new age of information and access?

This issue of the *Journal of Media and Religion* looks at how religion is framed when it is thrust into the public realm through mediated coverage of a particular event. The first article by Cynthia A. McCune examines how the public debate about teaching evolution was framed by the press in Tennessee. The way journalists presented religious and secular voices in this public debate is examined through a triangulation of methods. McCune argues that a number of involved parties shape news coverage, not just the journalists involved. Next, Chiung Hwang Chen discusses framing of news stories about Mormons during the 2002 Winter Olympic

Games in Salt Lake City. The Olympics were seen by some as an opportunity for the Mormon Church to clarify its beliefs and enhance its image through media coverage. Using the concept of "model minority discourse," Chen concludes that many of the stereotypes applied to Mormons in the past were not erased by the excitement of the games. Many framing patterns persist with regard to covering Mormons. The final article by Rick Clifton Moore applies Silk's (1995) unsecular media hypothesis to coverage of the Jesse Jackson infidelity scandal. His research explores whether journalists framed their stories in ways that ultimately promoted a religious worldview.

Each of these articles uncovers new issues and insights about the framing of religion news. We hope that they will become important points of departure for theorization on this important topic. Future research will benefit from the analyses presented by these authors.

REFERENCES

Buddenbaum, J. M. (1998). *Reporting news about religion: An introduction for journalists*. Ames: Iowa State University Press.

Evensen, B. (2000). The mass media and revivalism in the Gilded Age. In W. D. Sloan (Ed.), *Media and religion in American history* (pp. 119–133). Northport, AL: Vision Press.

Goffman, E. (1974). *Frame analysis: An essay on the organization of experience*. Cambridge, MA: Harvard University Press.

Lasswell, H. (1971). *Propaganda technique in the world war*. Cambridge, MA: MIT Press.

Meyrowitz, J. (1994). Medium theory. In D. Crowley & D. Mitchell (Eds.), *Communication theory today* (pp. 50–77). Stanford, CA: Stanford University Press.

Olasky, M. (1990). Democracy and the secularization of the American press. In Q. J. Schultze (Ed.), *American evangelicals and the mass media* (pp. 47–68). Grand Rapids, MI: Academie/Zondervan.

Schement, J. R., & Stephenson, H. C. (1996). Religion and the information society. In D. A. Stout & J. M. Buddenbaum (Eds.), *Religion and mass media: Audiences and adaptations* (pp. 261–289). Thousand Oaks, CA: Sage.

Silk, M. (1995). *Unsecular media: Making news of religion in America*. Urbana: University of Illinois Press.

Sloan, W. D. (2000). The origins of the American newspaper. In W. D. Sloan (Ed.), *Media and religion in American history* (pp. 32–53). Northport, AL: Vision Press.

Williams, J. H. (2000). Evangelism and the genesis of printing in America. In W. D. Sloan (Ed.), *Media and religion in American history* (pp. 1–16). Northport, AL: Vision Press.

JOURNAL OF MEDIA AND RELIGION, 2(1), 5–28

ARTICLES

Framing Reality: Shaping the News Coverage of the 1996 Tennessee Debate on Teaching Evolution

Cynthia A. McCune

School of Journalism and Mass Communications
San Jose State University

This study triangulated research methods to analyze how the public debate on a controversial issue was framed, and by whom, as a means of understanding the process and outcome of that debate. Its findings support the idea that public debates are framed by all involved parties, not just the news media. It also considered how the relative power position held by each side in this debate may have affected their interactions with the news media.

The 1996 Tennessee legislative debate on teaching evolution offered an opportunity to analyze how public debate on a controversial issue was framed, and by whom, as a way to better understand both the process and the outcome of that debate.

This issue may, at first, seem to be so unusual that its framing would not be relevant to debates on other public issues. However, the continuing evolution controversy is part of a larger public debate that expresses a deep-seated cultural conflict that divides large segments of the American public.

Hunter (1991) defined cultural conflict as "political and social hostility rooted in different systems of moral understanding" (p. 42). At the heart of debates over issues such as school prayer, sex education, homosexuality, and abortion is a clash between two incompatible worldviews. Hunter described these opposing views as "the impulse toward orthodoxy and the impulse toward progressivism" (p. 43).

Requests for reprints should be sent to Cynthia A. McCune, 3177 Greenoak Court, San Mateo, CA 94403. E-mail: cynmccune@aol.com

As Hunter and others (e.g., Nelkin, 1995) have noted, the news media is a primary arena for public debate on cultural conflicts. Debates on public issues can be viewed as symbolic contests over which interpretation will prevail (Gamson & Modigliani, 1989).

BACKGROUND

With the February 8, 1996, introduction of Senate Bill 3229, the Tennessee legislature again took up the issue of teaching evolution in public schools. As debate began in the Senate Education Committee, the bill was reported in the media and began to get the attention of both the public and the advocacy groups that would oppose it.

The proposed legislation was quickly dubbed "the monkey bill" because it recalled for many the legendary 1925 Scopes trial in which a Tennessee schoolteacher, John T. Scopes, was found guilty of teaching evolution to high school students. Thus began the battle of competing news frames, as the defenders of orthodoxy squared off against the proponents of progressivism in the Tennessee legislature and in the media.

Tennessee's 1925 law banning the teaching of evolution remained on the books until 1967. In 1973, the Tennessee General Assembly passed a new statute requiring that evolution could only be taught as a theory, not as a fact, and that "equal time" must be given to other creation theories "including, but not limited to, the Genesis account in the Bible" (Nelkin, 1977, p. 51).

A state appeals court overruled the 1973 legislation 2 years later, placing a damper on similar bills in other states. However, in 1980, Republican presidential candidate Ronald Reagan gave new life to the issue when he endorsed the equal time concept (Berra, 1990, p. 123; Larson, 1989, p. 126; Wills, 1990, p. 120).

In 1981, a federal judge overturned another version of the equal time approach, the Arkansas Balanced Treatment Act. In 1987, the U.S. Circuit Court of Appeals ruled against the Louisiana Creationism Act, which also attempted to legislate equal time in public school classrooms for teaching evolution and creationism. However, religious conservatives have continued their fight against teaching evolution in public schools.

Like the 1973 law, the 1996 bill would not have completely banned the teaching of evolution. However, it would have prohibited evolution from being taught as a fact in the state's public schools.

The ensuing public debate lasted less than 2 months. The debate involved politics, religion, the state's image, public education, and science, in roughly that order. In fact, state legislators "devoted more effort to warning of [the bill's] public-relations impact than to defending the theory of evolution" (Larson, 1997, p. 263). Although the Tennessee bill was defeated, conflicts over issues such as this are never really over as long as the underlying cultural clash remains. Since 1996, bills to limit the teaching of evolution have been debated in Ohio, Georgia, and North Carolina (Dubay, 1997).

Literature Review

For the past 25 or 30 years, mass communication studies have focused largely on media effects, framing, and agenda setting. From the writings of Cohen to those of McCombs, researchers have focused on the news media's role in framing and setting the news agenda for public issues.

However, some recent studies (e.g., Gamson & Wolfsfeld, 1993; Liebler & Bendix, 1996; Robinson & Powell, 1996) have recognized that political advocates and social movements have become increasingly sophisticated at influencing how the media frame public debates. This makes it critical to look beyond the media when assessing how a public debate was framed.

A number of researchers (e.g., Andsager, 2000; Gamson & Modigliani, 1989; Gamson & Wolfsfeld, 1993; Hansen, 1991; Robinson & Powell, 1996) have gone beyond content and frame analysis to consider who influences how issues are framed by the media. Instead of simply viewing the media as the primary agent that frames public issues and sets the public agenda, these researchers also view the media as a venue in which groups with conflicting worldviews attempt to establish their perspective as dominant. In other words, they regard the news media both as an influential group and as a group that is subject to influence.

From this perspective, which is exemplified by Neuman, Just, and Crigler's (1992) constructionist model of political communication, all key players in a public debate on a policy issue—political advocates, the media, and the public—are actively involved in framing the debate and in constructing what is perceived to be the reality of the situation.

Other researchers, including Carey (1989), have emphasized the role of symbolism in shaping public perceptions, and the ways in which institutions, political parties, and social movements use symbols to help define issues and persuade the public. Gamson and Modigliani (1989) described debates on public policy issues as "symbolic contests" over which interpretation will prevail. Gamson and Wolfsfeld (1993) also spoke of framing as a negotiation over meaning conducted among social movements and media.

Robinson and Powell (1996), for example, drew on Gamson's research for their analysis of competing reality frames in the 1991 Senate Judiciary Committee hearings on Clarence Thomas. They concluded that whoever most effectively frames the debate usually wins the debate.

Petersen and Markle (1989) discussed how resonances add familiarity and salience to news frames, and Petty and Priester (1994) suggested how the use of cultural symbols and resonances can influence the attitudes of even the politically uninvolved. Danielian (1992) noted that in political debate over social issues, interest groups often play a major role in making an issue salient to both policymakers and the media.

Several other recent studies have taken a similar approach (e.g., Gamson & Wolfsfeld, 1993; Liebler & Bendix, 1996; Neuman et al., 1992; Robinson & Powell, 1996) to examine how advocates and social movements use legislation and the news media to "frame" reality and advance their own worldviews.

To paraphrase Carey (1989), this study of the 1996 Tennessee evolution debate examines how the participants in a public debate attempted to define reality in terms of their own worldviews through the use of symbols and social values and through their use of the media. It also shows, as Hansen (1991) observed and as Robinson and Powell (1996) demonstrated, that it is more enlightening to map how public issues are articulated and how meaning is constructed than it is simply to try to determine whether the media influences public opinion, or vice versa.

Analysis of the Tennessee legislative debate also confirms Petersen and Markle's (1989) and Gamson and Wolfsfeld's (1993) observations on how a social movement's power position affects its interactions with the media. They noted that the side in power usually tries to limit the scope of the debate, whereas the underdog tries to broaden the debate and involve third parties. This pattern was reflected in the Tennessee debate.

Research Questions

Key questions in this study were the following: Which frames dominated the news coverage of this debate? How was this debate framed, and by whom? Were popular cultural symbols and social values used to create resonances and add salience to news frames? Was one side in this debate more successful in framing this issue in terms of its own worldview? Did the media interactions of those involved in this debate follow the power position patterns observed by Petersen and Markle (1989) and Gamson and Wolfsfeld (1993)?

METHOD

Quantitative methods of analysis provided a foundation of hard data for this study, and qualitative sources and methods added depth and corroboration. Triangulation of multiple research methods and sources provided multiple measures of the same phenomenon and converging lines of inquiry that helped substantiate the findings.

Quantitative methods used for this study included content and framing analysis of the news coverage of the 1996 legislation. Data sources included 62 news articles, features, editorials, and commentaries on this issue that ran in the state's three largest daily newspapers, as well as in a smaller daily that served the district of one of the bill's sponsors.

The newspapers were selected because of their prominence within the state, as indicated by their circulation figures and statewide distribution. They are also representative of the state's three distinct geographic, cultural, and political regions. A fourth, smaller daily was also added to the sample as a form of negative case testing. As the hometown paper of the legislation's senate sponsor, it might reflect a somewhat different news perspective. Newspapers used for this study are:

- *The Commercial Appeal* of Memphis, with a circulation of approximately 188,700 on weekdays and 267,900 on Sundays.
- The *Knoxville News Sentinel,* with a circulation of approximately 115,600 on weekdays and 167,500 on Sundays.
- *The Tennessean* of Nashville, with a circulation of approximately 146,750 on weekdays and 281,900 on Sundays.
- *The Herald Citizen* of Cookeville, with a circulation of approximately 11,000 daily and 13,275 on Sundays.

Tennessee has a variety of geographic and cultural influences. East Tennessee is the least ethnically diverse part of the state, as well as the most politically conservative and most Republican region of the state. Its biggest city, Knoxville, is home to the *Knoxville News Sentinel.* West Tennessee consists of flatland plains, bordered on the west by the Mississippi River. Its largest city, Memphis, is home to the *Commercial Appeal,* as well as to Elvis's Graceland. West Tennessee has a more ethnically diverse population than the other parts of the state. Politically, it is more Democratic.

The *Tennessean* is headquartered in Nashville, the state capital, in central Tennessee. Politically, the central region of the state falls between the political extremes of east and west. The small daily selected for this sample is also located in central Tennessee; Cookeville is about 50 miles east of Nashville.

Qualitative data sources for this study included focused interviews, documentary evidence, and archival documents. Qualitative measures used for this study included pattern matching and reduction through qualitative content coding.

Fifteen people were interviewed for this study: four legislators who were directly involved in the debate (one pro, two con, and one mixed); three political advocates who were frequently quoted in the news articles used in this study (one pro and two con); and eight reporters (see Table 1) who covered the legislative debate for the newspapers used in this study. One of the bill's sponsors, Senator Tommy Burks, did not respond to initial requests for an interview. A few months later he was killed by a political rival.

Quantitative Coding and Levels of Analysis

This study used two levels of quantitative analysis: the overall article and the major news frames and their sources.

TABLE 1
Reporters Who Covered the 1996 Tennessee Debate on Evolution

The Commercial Appeal, Memphis, Tennessee	
*Paula Wade, Nashville Bureau	5 news articles
AP—non-bylined	3 news articles
*Richard Locker, Nashville bureau chief	2 news articles
Sarah A. Derks (education)	1 news article
Jody Callahan, general assignment reporter	1 news article
The Herald Citizen, Cookeville, Tennessee	
*AP—Vicki Brown byline	5 news articles
AP—non-bylined	5 news articles
Advertorials (church commentary ads)	2 advertorials
*Mary Jo Denton, staff writer	1 news article
Knoxville News Sentinel, Knoxville, Tennessee	
*Tom Humphrey, Nashville bureau	3 news articles
*Jesse Fox Mayshark, staff writer (UT beat)	2 news articles
*AP—Vicki Brown byline	2 news articles
Editorial page writer	2 editorials
Rebecca Ferrar, Nashville bureau	1 news article
Frank Cagle, staff writer/columnist (state government)	1 column (half on this issue)
David Hunter, local columnist	1 column
Theotis Robinson, local columnist	1 column
The Tennessean, Nashville, Tennessee	
*Duren Cheek, staff writer (state government)	12 news articles
*Ray Waddle, religion editor	3 news articles/1 column
Larry Daughrey, staff writer (state government)	3 news articles
Editorial page writer	3 editorials
Lisa Benavides, staff writer (education)	1 news article
Diane Long, feature writer	1 feature article
Catherine Darnell, staff writer/columnist	1 column (first person)
Guest columnist	1 guest column

Note. Reporters who covered this issue for the four newspapers included in this study are listed by newspaper, in order of the number of articles written. Reporters who were interviewed for this study are indicated by an asterisk.

All articles were coded for several variables at the first stage of analysis. These include the following nominal variables: the newspaper in which the article appeared (*Commercial Appeal, Herald Citizen, News Sentinel, The Tennessean*); its publication date (e.g., March 21, 1996); the type of article (general news article, feature article, editorial, etc.); two indicators of the article's prominence, its placement (front page, second front, editorial page, inside page, etc.) and its length (word count); and the main focus of the article (overall topics that are related to likely frames).

Also included in this stage of analysis were several variables using ordinal measures. These included the tone of the headline, the tone of the overall article, and the tone of any accompanying photograph or illustration. The following scale was used for these measures: 1 (*very favorable*; i.e., strongly favors the legislation), 2 (*fa-*

vorable), 3 (*neither favorable nor unfavorable*), 4 (*unfavorable*), and 5 (*very unfavorable; i.e.*, strongly opposes the legislation).

The second stage of analysis focused on news frames, using frames as the unit of analysis. In all, 25 separate news frames were identified for this study, not including the "other" category. Coders identified all major news frames appearing in each article included in the study, based on definitions developed by the researcher.

Frames were also grouped into three categories, according to their orientation toward the legislation and their usage: Pro frames are those that were used by the bill's proponents in support of the legislation; con frames were used by the bill's opponents against the legislation; and mixed frames were used either by both sides or by reporters to provide context.

Source Types

Each frame was also coded for type of sources to help determine who framed the debate. Sources were defined as individuals or groups who were quoted or paraphrased in the articles (or the editorial writer, columnist, or reporter, in cases of unattributed frames or editorial commentary).

Source types were further identified by their attitude toward the legislation. Sources favorable to the legislation were identified as pro, those unfavorable toward it were identified as con, and those that neither favored nor opposed the legislation were identified as neither or neutral. For example, a legislator who supported the bill was coded as pro/legislator, whereas one who opposed it was a con/legislator, and one who straddled the fence on the issue was a neutral/legislator. This system of coding made it possible to readily differentiate sources who supported the legislation from those who opposed it.

FINDINGS AND DISCUSSION

Except in the opening week of the legislative debate, the frame analysis showed that negative frames (those opposing the legislation) dominated the news coverage of this debate in the four newspapers studied by a nearly three-to-one margin (see Table 2).

The debate was largely framed by legislators and political advocates. These included Representative Zane Whitson and Senator Burks, the bill's cosponsors; Senator Steve Cohen, a liberal senator; Senator Andy Womack, the chair of the Senate Education Committee; and lobbyists for the Tennessee chapter of the American Civil Liberties Union (ACLU), the Tennessee Education Association (TEA), and the Tennessee Christian Coalition (TCC).

Both sides in this debate attempted to use popular cultural symbols and social values to create resonances supporting their perspectives on this issue. For exam-

TABLE 2
Frames Predominating in the News Coverage

| | Weeks | | | | | | | |
Frame Category	1 and 2	3	4	5	6	7	8	Totals
Pro frames (favorable)	6	9	42	11	1	7	9	85
Con frames (unfavorable)	5	17	99	34	22	30	33	240
Mixed frames (neither/both)	5	3	43	14	6	6	24	101
Totals	16	29	184	59	29	43	66	426

Note. Weeks 1 and 2 were combined because only three articles appeared during this period and all focused generally on the evolution bill's introduction.

ple, the bill's supporters said that they were trying to protect children and families, and argued that morals, values, and telling the truth were the real issues at stake. They also used the concept of equal time, which draws on the values of fairness and equality, in support of the bill, and used the Bible as a symbol of the rightness of their cause. However, the bill's supporters were somewhat limited in this regard by their desire to downplay the bill's religious underpinnings.

The bill's opponents had no such limits. They took advantage of the state's history as the site of the 1925 Scopes trial to exploit concerns about the bill's potential impact on the state's image and economy. They used the monkey bill nickname to ridicule the bill, and used popular cultural symbols and social values to create resonances and add salience to their views. In addition, they also co-opted a favorite conservative issue, local control.

The bill's cosponsors, Representative Whitson and Senator Burks, acted as though they held the power position in this debate. From a legal perspective, this was a questionable tactic because previous high court rulings put their bill on shaky ground. Culturally, however, the dominant power approach was reasonable because Tennessee has a well-deserved reputation as a secure notch in the nation's Bible Belt.

For the most part, the bill's sponsors attempted to limit the scope of the debate and did not actively seek allies. For example, Jon Crisp, then director of the TCC, said the bill's sponsors did not consult with the TCC prior to the bill's introduction or seek his help in getting it passed.

The bill's opponents appeared to act from a low-power position. Two influential senators and ACLU and TEA lobbyists tried to broaden the scope of the debate and bring third parties into the debate. In particular, the ACLU worked to involve others as allies. Hedy Weinberg, director of the Tennessee ACLU, said her organization strategized ways to frame the legislation to encourage other individuals and groups, such as scientists, educators, and the business community, to speak out against it.

The bill's opponents did a better job of framing the debate in terms of their own worldviews. Because of their success in broadening the scope of the debate, the public debate over the 1996 Tennessee evolution bill was dominated by the voices and frames of the opposition.

Overview of the News Coverage and Coding

The 1996 evolution bill was debated in the Tennessee legislature for about 8 weeks. It was introduced February 8, 1996, and voted down on March 28, 1996. During this period, 62 news articles, features, editorials, and other commentaries relating to the legislation appeared in the four newspapers studied. All 62 news articles were coded for news frames and the sources of those frames, in addition to other salient coding categories such as the type of article, placement, and tone.

As indicated in Table 3, news coverage of this issue peaked in Week 4, when the bill was considered by the full Senate after its approval by the Senate Education Committee. At this point, all parties involved in the debate—including the news media—began taking the bill more seriously.

In particular, it is interesting to note the change over time in the overall tone of the news coverage. The tone of the first week of coverage was neutral—neither favorable nor unfavorable toward the bill. After that, news coverage gradually became more negative, except for a slight moderation in Week 5, until the legislation was voted down.

In the four newspapers studied, negative or con news frames (those unfavorable to the bill) dominated the news coverage of this legislation in all but the first week. As shown in Table 2 and in Figure 1, negative frames outnumbered positive frames (those favoring the bill) by a nearly three-to-one margin. Mixed frames—those that were more neutral or used by both sides—also slightly outnumbered positive frames. The majority of mixed frames came from reporters providing background information on the 1925 Scopes trial as context for the 1996 debate. Much of that

TABLE 3
Overview of the Volume and Tone of News Coverage

	Weeks						
Variable	1 and 2	3	4	5	6	7	8
Word counts	1,030	2,594	12,684	5,026	2,997	4,157	4,636
No. of articles	3	5	22	10	5	6	10
Tone[a] (average)	3.3	3.4	3.7	3.5	4.2	4.0	3.8[b]
No. of editorials and columns	0	0	6	1	2	1	1
Tone[a] of editorials	NA	NA	4.7	5	5	4	3[b]

Note. Weeks 1 and 2 were combined because only three articles appeared during this period and all focused generally on the bill's introduction. NA = not applicable.

[a]The overall tone of each article was ranked on a scale of 1 to 5, where 1 was *strongly favorable toward the legislation*, 2 was *favorable*, 3 was *neither favorable nor unfavorable*, 4 was *unfavorable*, and 5 was *strongly unfavorable*. [b]In Week 8, following the bill's defeat, its opponents became somewhat magnanimous and more neutral in tone.

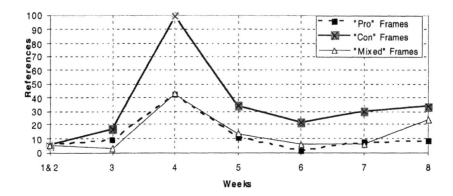

FIGURE 1   Week-by-week graph of pro, con, and mixed news frames. In the four newspapers studied, a total of 425 frames were used in the news coverage of and editorializing about this issue. The number of frames peaked—along with the number of articles published—in Week 4, which had 184 frames.

information was presented in Weeks 4 and 5, after the bill was sent to the full Senate for consideration.

Not surprisingly, news sources showed a similar trend. Except during the first 2 weeks of news coverage, significantly more opponents than proponents of the bill were quoted in the newspapers studied. Overall, con news sources (those opposing the bill) outnumbered pro news sources (those favoring the bill) by nearly three to one. Even when source comparisons were limited to those cited in news and feature articles (omitting editorials and other opinion pieces, which were mostly negative), reporters used approximately two thirds more con than pro sources on this issue.

This predominance of opposing sources and negative frames could indicate any number of things, including the following: a liberal media bias; a lack of grassroots support for the bill; inadequate political strategy, organization, and commitment on the part of the bill's sponsors; or the superior political strategy, organization, and commitment of the bill's opponents. In this case, it appears the dominance of negative news frames and news sources was due to the superior organization, strategy, and coalition-building efforts of the bill's opponents.

The findings of the newspaper framing analysis, combined with qualitative data from interviews with the legislators, lobbyists, and reporters who were involved in this debate, show how this issue was framed and by whom.

The data clearly show that con frames dominated the newspaper coverage of this debate, indicating that the bill's opponents did a better job of framing this issue in terms of their worldviews. The data also indicate which side in this debate was working from the political and cultural power position in its dealings with the media and the legislature, and which side was not. Finally, the findings show how and why the 1996 evolution bill was defeated in the Tennessee legislature.

Overview of News Frames

I initially identified 26 separate frames used to describe this legislation during the course of the debate. A total of 425 frames were identified and coded in the 62 articles reviewed for this study.

Frame classification.   Frames were classified two ways: by number of references and by attitude toward the proposed legislation. According to the total number of references they received in the articles surveyed, frames were classified as dominant (31–40 references), major (21–30 references), moderate (11–20 references), or minor (5–10 references). Any frame with less than 5 references was coded as "other."

Frames favorable toward the legislation were classified as pro, and those unfavorable toward the legislation were classified as con. Those that were neither favorable nor unfavorable or were used by both sides in the debate were classified as mixed frames. In total, there were 13 unfavorable or con frames, 8 favorable or pro frames, and 5 mixed frames including the "other" category (see the Appendix).

In this debate, all dominant and major frames were unfavorable. As shown in Table 4, the Scopes or history frame (40 references), the monkey bill frame (39 references), and the state's image frame (33 references) each received more than 30 mentions, making them the dominant frames in this debate. (See Table 5 for a summary of pro and con "competing reality" frames.) Three frames—right-wing politics (27 references), unconstitutional (27 references), and intimidate teachers (24 references)—received 21 to 30 references each, putting them in the major frame category. A total of 25 references were tallied in the "other" frame category. Eight frames fell in the moderate category with 11 to 20 references each, and 11 frames had 5 to 10 references, putting them in the minor frame category (see Table 4).

Negative frames.   The most influential frames used by those who opposed the legislation were the monkey bill frame (39 references), which derisively labeled and linked the 1996 bill to the original 1925 monkey law; the state's image frame (33 references), which asserted the bill was making the state look foolish and would hinder its economic development efforts; the right-wing politics frame (27 references), which alleged the bill was either the result of religious conservatives throwing their political weight around, or that it was intended to win support from religious conservatives for the bill's sponsors; the unconstitutional frame (27 references), which said the bill was trying to circumvent the separation of church and state; and the intimidate teachers frame (24 references), which described the bill as an attempt to intimidate teachers into avoiding teaching.

TABLE 4
Frames by Category[a], Listed in Order of (Number of) References

Con Frames[b]	Pro Frames[c]	Mixed Frames[d]
Dominant frames (31–40)		
Monkey bill (39)		Scopes/history (40)
State's image (33)		
Major frames (21–30)		
Right-wing politics (27)		"Other" frames (25)
Unconstitutional (27)		
Intimidate teachers (24)		
Moderate frames (11–20)		
Mandate/local control (17)	Morals/values/truth (20)	Evolution vs. biblical
Ridicule of the bill (15)	"Not a fact" (19)	creationism (16)
Education (11)	Protect children (12)	
Agriculture and micro–macro evolution (11)		
Minor frames (5–10)		
Confusing bill (10)	Equal time (9)	God/bible (10)
Cost (9)	Christian rights (7)	Theory (10)
Radical right (8)	"It's a serious bill" (7)	
Evolution/science (8)	Secular/atheists (5)	
	Overzealous teachers (5)	

Note. A total of 425 frames were identified in the 62 articles included in this study.
[a]Frames were categorized by their attitude toward the legislation. Con frames were unfavorable (or opposed) to the evolution bill; pro frames favored (or supported) the bill; and mixed frames were either neutral or those that were used by both sides in the debate. [b]n = 240. [c]n = 84. [d]n = 101.

Frames most frequently used by the bill's supporters were: the morals, values, and truth frame (20 references) and the "not a fact" frame (19 references). The morals frame asserts that the bill is about morals, values, and telling the truth. The "truth" part of the morals frame also relates to another frequently used pro frame, the "not a fact" frame, which asserted that evolution is a theory, not a fact. These frames were sometimes used together, as when the bill's supporters said teachers should tell students the truth, which is that evolution is not a fact.

The morals, values, and truth frame was sometimes combined with the "protect children" frame (12 references), which said children are easily influenced and should be protected from exposure to misinformation that could damage their moral development. Another frame used by the bill's supporters was the equal time frame (9 references), which argued it was unfair to allow the theory of evolution to be taught but not the theory of creation. This frame was introduced by a spokesman for the TCC.

Frames categorized as mixed did not clearly support or oppose the legislation. This includes frames used by both sides in this debate, including some that could be

TABLE 5
Competing Reality Frames in the 1996 Debate on Teaching Evolution

Pro Frames (The Bill's Supporters) "It's About Values"	Con Frames (The Bill's Opponents) "It Makes Us Look Foolish"
What they said about the bill:	*What they said about the bill:*
It's about morals, values, and the truth	It's damaging the state's image and threatening the
It's about teaching evolution as a theory, not a	state's economy
fact	It's ridiculous, Neanderthal, and a throwback to the
It's about protecting children	1920s
It's about equal time and fairness	It's about right-wing politics
It's about stopping overzealous teachers	It's unconstitutional
It's about the rights of Christian parents to have a	It's about intimidating teachers
say in education	It's a state mandate
	It would cost too much
	It's confusing
What they said about the other side:	*What they said about the other side:*
They're nonbelievers	They're radical, right-wing Christian conservatives
They're secular humanists and atheists	They're interfering with local control of public
They're promoting the religion of secular	schools
humanism in our classrooms	They're trying to bring religion into our classrooms
They're trying to impose their beliefs on our	They're trying to impose their beliefs on our
children	children

interpreted as either supporting or opposing the legislation, depending on the reader's point of view (see the Appendix for frame descriptions).

The Scopes or history frame (40 references), which refers to the 1925 Scopes trial and the history of the evolution debate, was classified as a mixed frame because it was most often used by reporters to provide context and background for news stories on this issue. However, for many people the Scopes trial carried a negative connotation.

Another mixed frame, the evolution and creationism frame (16 references), was also used to provide context for this debate. It discussed the basis of conflicts between evolution and biblical creationism. Two other mixed frames, the theory frame (10 references) and the God and Bible frame (10 references), were used by both sides in this debate. Because of this joint usage, these frames tended to cancel each other out; they were not very effective for either side.

Chronology of News Coverage

The first news coverage came February 9, when *The Tennessean* and *Herald Citizen* ran articles on the bill's introduction. Both articles compared the evolution bill to the state's 1925 monkey law, setting the underlying tone for much of the future discussion of the bill. These articles also set another more short-lived precedent: Both quoted more people who favored the bill than were opposed to it. This was the only week when pro news sources outnumbered con news sources in the four newspapers studied.

Although the first two articles focused on the evolution bill itself, over the next 2 weeks the evolution bill was sometimes lumped together with two other morals bills also under debate in the Tennessee legislature: the Ten Commandments resolution, which would have required posting the Ten Commandments in the state's public buildings; and a bill proposing a ban on same-sex marriage. The Ten Commandments bill had already attracted national media attention.

The turning point.   The evolution bill got its first hearing in the Senate Education Committee on Febrary 21, 3 weeks after its introduction. Several state senators raised concerns about how it was written, because the bill did not clearly define evolution or provide for due process for teachers accused of teaching evolution as fact. Senator Roscoe Dixon said it was "not even grammatically correct" (Tennessee Senate Education Committee, 1996). In spite of these concerns, the bill was approved eight to one by the education committee and sent to the full Senate for its consideration. The lone dissenting vote came from the committee chairman, Senator Andy Womack.

After the bill's approval by the Senate Education Committee, negative news frames and sources began to edge out positive news frames and sources in the newspapers studied. This trend began in Week 3, as reporters wrote about the bill's initial passage, and accelerated in Week 4, as the bill was taken up by the full Senate. During Weeks 3 and 4, six new negative news frames appeared while only one new positive frame appeared.

News coverage peaked in Week 4, as editorial writers and columnists began addressing the issue. For example, the *News Sentinel* and *The Tennessean* ran six opinion pieces on this issue: four editorials and two columns. Five of them strongly opposed the bill; the sixth column, by *The Tennessean*'s religion editor, was a more neutral piece that discussed why evolution is viewed as such a threat by religious conservatives and how religious liberals could better position themselves in public debates on social values (Waddle, 1996, p. 2D).

Of the 11 opinion pieces that appeared on this issue during the legislative debate, 9 strongly opposed the legislation and 2 were neutral, focusing on the issues behind the debate. There were no editorials in favor of the legislation. Senator Cohen attributed the bill's defeat to "the public debate in the newspapers, and the strong commentary ... saying this was going to make us a laughingstock." He said, "It was embarrassing" (S. Cohen, personal communication, August 18, 1998).

During the final 4 weeks of the legislative debate, from March 4 through March 31, negative news frames outnumbered positive frames in all the newspapers studied.

Framing the Debate

Several significant themes in this debate were introduced in the first 2 weeks of news coverage. The bill's cosponsors established five frames when they introduced the bill. They asserted the legislation was needed because overzealous teachers were telling impressionable children that evolution is a proven fact, even though it is just a theory. They also asserted that the proposed legislation would be constitutional, because it did not actually ban the teaching of evolution, just the teaching of evolution as a fact.

Asked by a reporter to comment on the bill, John Hannah, chairman emeritus of the TCC, introduced the equal time frame. He asserted that it was unfair to allow the theory of evolution to be taught if the theory of biblical creation could not also be taught.

Hedy Weinberg, director of the Tennessee ACLU, was the first person to speak out against the bill. She characterized it as an attempt to "intimidate teachers" into avoiding the topic of evolution in their classrooms. Raising the Scopes or history frame, she said, "I would certainly hope that the Monkey Trial, as it was referred to in the '20s, is not played out again in Tennessee in 1996" (Cheek, 1996b, p. 1A). That same article also cited other critics of the bill as saying it had all the makings of a modern-day monkey law, introducing what quickly became the monkey bill frame.

It was inevitable that opponents would compare the 1996 evolution bill to the state's 1925 monkey law, and the 1996 legislative debate to 1925 Scopes trial. It was therefore no surprise that the Scopes or history frame, at 40 references, was the most frequently used frame in this debate. It was also the only one that appeared in every week of the debate.

Unfortunately for the bill's supporters, the Scopes or history frame carried negative connotations for many people. Although this frame was introduced by the bill's opponents, it was included in the mixed frame category because it was mainly used by reporters providing background or contextual information on the history of the evolution debate in Tennessee.

The negative connotations of the Scopes or history frame provided a foundation for several other unfavorable news frames, including the monkey bill, state's image, and ridicule frames. These frames were both complementary and synergistic. All three suggested the 1996 evolution bill, like the 1925 monkey law, was foolish and would make the state look bad.

The state's image and ridicule frames were fueled by the national and international media attention the bill received. A *Commercial Appeal* news article quoting Senator Cohen in Week 2 also laid the groundwork for the state's image frame, which appeared in Week 3, when it noted that the evolution bill had "made national news, much to the chagrin of many legislators" (Wade, 1996, p. 1B).

Two days after the bill was passed out of the Education Committee and sent to the full Senate, *The New York Times* published an article on the Ten Commandments bill and also briefly discussed the evolution bill (Applebaum, 1996a). The media frenzy had begun. As the ACLU's Weinberg noted:

> You had the BBC down here; you had Russian stations and Australian stations calling all of us and the legislators for comments … all over the country you had the media talking to legislators about what this bill was about and what the impact was. And I think the legislators—certainly the leaders in the House and Senate—began to understand that this could have a greater impact than they realized, and that they had to get hold of it. (personal communication, August 7, 1998)

Nationally, for example, *The Christian Science Monitor* (Spaid, 1996) and *The New York Times* (Applebaum, 1996b) published front-page stories on conservative Christians' renewed efforts to have creationism taught in the public schools, using the Tennessee bill as an example. *USA Today* also ran a feature on the bill (Curley, 1996). An editorial in *The Tennessean* noted that the ABC *Nightly News* and *The Today Show* had recently reported on the bill. The editorial writer expressed concern that "if the bill becomes law, the jesting and national jokes about Tennessee and its lawmakers will surely escalate" ("Inherit the Wind," 1996).

Dealing with the media.   Representative Whitson was "amazed" by the amount of media attention the bill received. "I got calls from all over the world on it," he said (personal communication, July 31, 1998).

At first, Whitson was receptive to giving interviews to the national news media, but he said the media's ridicule of the bill eventually prompted him to stop. The bill's opponents and some reporters "made a mockery of it," he said. "It was the Monkey Bill all over again. I think they were unfair in playing it up as the Scopes thing" (personal communication, August 21, 1998). The bill's cosponsor, Senator Burks, avoided talking to the national news media from the start.

The bill's opponents benefited from the national and international media attention the bill attracted. They used that news coverage to bolster the credibility of the state's image and ridicule frames, and to create concern about the bill's potential impact on the state's economy. As the ACLU's Weinberg commented:

> It kind of worked to our advantage that we had more media coverage, which allowed us the luxury of using those arguments … that this is going to affect the business community, that Tennessee is going to become a laughingstock, [and that] 70 years later we're still fighting the same battle. … There's no question that the major media attention that we got, for good or bad, influenced some of the legislators' votes. (personal communication, August 7, 1998)

The bill's opponents mobilize.   By Week 3, when the bill was approved by the Senate Education Committee, its opponents had begun to mobilize. They introduced five new frames—including the state's image frame and the unconstitutional frame. Supporters generated just one new frame, the morals, values, and truth frame. Earlier in the week, before the Education Committee discussed the bill, Senator Cohen initiated the state's image frame by saying this type of legislation "gives Tennessee a bad name ... [and] makes us look foolish to the rest of the country" (Cheek, 1996a, p. 1B).

As *News Sentinel* reporter Jesse Mayshark commented, "The people opposed to [the bill] were much more effective ... in broadening the issue to this whole question of Tennessee's standing as part of the 'New South' and as a progressive state" (personal communication, July 31, 1998).

After the bill was passed out of the Education Committee over his objections, Senator Womack publicly voiced his concerns about local control, pointing out the bill would let the legislature set school curriculums. This quickly evolved into the mandate and local control frame, co-opting both the language and the symbolism of political conservatives, who had made local control and unfunded federal mandates a campaign issue in the 1994 elections.

In Weeks 3 and 4, the bill's supporters attempted to regain control of the debate by redefining the issue. The legislation, they said, was about morals, values, the truth, and about protecting children. In Week 4, the bill's opponents introduced four new frames, and its supporters introduced three new frames. Negative frames included the ridicule, education, confusing bill, and evolution and science frames. Positive frames included Christian rights, "it's a serious bill," and atheists and secular humanists frames.

The ridicule frame put the bill's supporters on the defensive. The new pro frames were mostly defensive, introduced by the bill's sponsors in response to the growing success of several negative frames. In one of these frames, Representative Whitson insisted that Christian parents have rights, too; in another, Senator Burks insisted that the evolution bill was not a joke. The third new pro frame, the atheists and secular humanists frame, attempted to label the bill's opponents as secular humanists or atheists, thus putting them at a disadvantage in a state where many voters are conservative Christians.

The ridicule frame first appeared February 26 in a *Tennessean* editorial that decried both the evolution bill and the Ten Commandments bill as "crude Neanderthal legislation." The editorial said, "By passing a new Monkey Bill and endorsing the Ten Commandments, Tennessee lawmakers are giving the entire state an image of hicks, rubes and yokels" ("Tennessee Lawmakers," 1996, p. 10A).

As the debate wore on, some newspaper columnists and a few reporters used humorous headlines and leads, perpetuating the ridicule frame. "The [Jay] Leno quotient was very high," commented *Commercial Appeal* reporter Paula Wade. "It was just such a fun story, who could resist?" (personal communication, August 14, 1998).

The emergence of the state's image and ridicule frames may have contributed to the introduction of another defensive frame, the Christian rights frame, in Week 4. This frame was typified by Representative Whitson's comment in defense of the bill: "Christian parents have rights. We live in a religious free country and those of us who believe in Christianity want our children to be able to think for themselves" (Cheek, 1996c, p. 1B).

The education frame started late, in Week 4, and persisted at a low level through the end of the debate. However, for the bill's opponents it represented a successful broadening of the debate and a mobilization of new groups against the bill. The three metro newspapers interviewed area teachers and professors about the bill's potential impact on education. Two of the newspapers studied ran articles when university faculty members spoke out against the bill.

Underlying the education frame was the concern that enacting the legislation would leave students ill-prepared for higher education and high-tech jobs, and that the reputation of the state's education system would be damaged. Those who used the education frame often linked it to the state's image frame.

Minor Frames

In addition to the equal time frame, other minor frames included the God and Bible frame, the evolution and science frame, and the theory frame. According to the numbers, the God and Bible frame, at 10 references, was a minor one in this debate. However, the social value of a shared belief in God and the cultural symbolism of the Bible formed the underpinnings of the morals, values, and truth frame, and lent resonance to that frame.

Commercial Appeal reporter Wade said:

> One thing that happens in debates like this, particularly where there is a so-called righteous point of view, is the labeling ... Either you're with the ACLU, those Godless communists, or you are with the good God-fearing believers. That's why it was so hard to kill ... I really do think labeling played a particularly big role in this [debate]. (personal communication, August 14, 1998)

However, because the bill's sponsors tried to frame the debate as an issue of fairness and values, not religion, to avoid raising constitutional questions relating to the separation of church and state, they generally avoided focusing on God and the Bible when talking about the evolution bill. The TCC, a politically savvy organization, also followed this model when discussing the bill.

During the final Senate vote on the bill, several senators invoked God as they cast their votes, either saying they were voting for their bill because of their belief in God and biblical creation, or professing their belief in God in spite of their vote against the bill.

"The people who did vote against it wanted to make very clear that they believed in God," said the ACLU's Hedy Weinberg. "There was a real desire on their part to say, 'I'm voting against it, but ... know that I believe in God'" (personal communication, August 8, 1998).

As the bill's supporters tried to avoid portraying the bill as religiously motivated, so the bill's opponents tried to avoid the monkey trap. "We did not intend to be drug into the issue of whether a man descended from a monkey," said TEA lobbyist Jerry Winters (personal communication, August 5, 1998).

Senator Womack, chair of the Senate Education Committee, said:

> I tried from the very beginning not to … get involved in the issue of evolution itself, but to deal with it as an issue of whether the legislature should be determining what and how subjects should be taught in school. (personal communication, August 17, 1998)

CONCLUSIONS

The findings of this thesis support the contention made by several researchers (e.g., Gamson & Wolfsfeld, 1993; Hansen, 1991) that all key players in a political debate, not just the media, are actively involved in interpreting and defining the issues.

The bill's sponsors linked their arguments in favor of the bill to several powerful symbols and related social values—including family values, God, and the Bible—that should have given them an advantage in a religiously and politically conservative state. Although perhaps operating at a cultural disadvantage in Tennessee, the bill's opponents benefited from having several articulate and politically savvy speakers for their cause. They also benefited from some colorful arguments: It's hard to compete with the catchiness and pure entertainment value of the monkey bill. In addition, they simply had more voices. They brought together more people and groups who were willing to speak up on their behalf than did the bill's supporters. This meant there were more readily available sources and story angles opposing the bill than there were favoring it.

Credibility and Replicability of Results

The small sample size (4 newspapers and 62 articles) limits the credibility of the findings of this study. However, triangulation of multiple sources of data and methods of analysis helps offset that disadvantage.

I originally planned to use Scott's pi to calculate intercoder reliability for this study. However, the complexity and sheer number of frame coding categories (26 possible frames and 22 possible sources) made that unfeasible. Instead, the admittedly less accurate Holsti formula for intercoder reliability was used. Using Holsti, the two coders of this study were found to be in 72% agreement on frames and sources only. This figure is somewhat low. In part, this is because the unit of analysis for this study was frames, not paragraphs, and because there was a catchall "other" frame category. This allowed for significant coder leeway in deciding what was and was not a frame—the source of nearly two thirds (64%) of intercoder disagreements.

Implications for Theory

This case study builds on recent mass communication and sociological studies (e.g., Gamson & Modigliani, 1989; Robinson & Powell, 1996; Taylor & Condit, 1988) that have used frame analysis to show how institutions, political advocates, and social movements use popular cultural symbols and social values to help sell their worldviews to the news media and the public. It illustrates, to use the terminology of Hansen (1991) and Gamson and Wolfsfeld (1993), how an issue was articulated and how meaning was constructed by those involved in a specific political debate. In addition, it confirms the media interaction patterns observed by Liebler and Bendix (1996) and Petersen and Markle (1989) in their studies of social movements involved in public policy debates.

This study also demonstrates the value of taking a more macrolevel approach to the question of media influence by looking beyond news frames and content to determine where those frames originated, as advocated by Lang and Lang (1981, 1983) and Robinson and Powell (1996). This may have been less of an issue in the 1970s, when agenda-setting theory was developed. However, as political institutions, politicians, and political advocacy groups have grown increasingly media savvy, it has become an important question in media studies. This is not to say that the media are without influence in public policy debates, but that the news media are not now, if they ever were, the primary influence on the way issues are framed.

A number of media scholars (e.g., Dalton, Beck, Huckfeldt, & Koetzle, 1998; Lang & Lang, 1981; Walters, Walters, & Gray, 1996) have criticized agenda-setting theory for its assumption that the mass media set the agenda for political campaigns. Likewise, this study questions that premise, and supports Liebler and Bendix's (1996) contention that "frames found in the news media may have their roots elsewhere" (p. 54)—including, as in this debate, in the information campaigns conducted by the opposing parties in a debate. It also supports Robinson and Powell's (1996) observation that the news media are most strongly influenced by the political players in a public debate.

In response to recent criticisms of agenda-setting theory, its practitioners have attempted to amend it. For example, a recent book on agenda setting (McCombs, Shaw, & Weaver, 1997) attempted to incorporate the concepts of framing, priming, and related psychological theories into a common theory of political communication.

Perhaps these repeated attempts to rework and shore up agenda-setting theory should be regarded in light of Kuhn's (1970) discussion of paradigm shifts in science. He said a paradigm shift can occur when normal, cumulative research is overtaken by the emergence of significant scientific anomalies that challenge the existing paradigm, or by new discoveries that cause researchers to reevaluate that paradigm. Kuhn also noted that the researchers who are most heavily invested in the current paradigm are often unwilling or unable to experience the conversion of viewpoint that comes with a paradigm shift. Instead, they resist change and try to forestall the overthrow of their favored theory. Eventually, however, if inconsistencies continue to accumulate and if other researchers continue to develop better explanations, the paradigm change will occur.

REFERENCES

Andsager, J. L. (2000). How interest groups attempt to shape public opinion with competing news frames. *Journalism & Mass Communication Quarterly, 77*, 577–592.

Applebaum, P. (1996a, February 23). Senate in Tennessee backs 10 Commandments' posting. *The New York Times*, p. 12A.

Applebaum, P. (1996b, March 10). 70 years after Scopes trial, creation debate lives. *The New York Times*, pp. 1, 12.

Berra, T. M. (1990). *Evolution and the myths of creationism: A basic guide to the facts in the evolution debate.* Stanford, CA: Stanford University Press.

Carey, J. W. (1989). *Communication as culture: Essays on media and society.* Boston: Unwin Hyman.

Cheek, D. (1996a, February 20). Bill aims to tighten loose morals. *The Tennessean*, pp. 1B, 2B.

Cheek, D. (1996b, February 9). Bill targets teaching of evolution as fact. *The Tennessean*, p. 1A.

Cheek, D. (1996c, February 28). Rules on teaching evolution pass. *The Tennessean*, p. 1B.

Curley, T. (1996, March 27). New life in evolution debate. *USA Today*, p. 3A.

Dalton, R. J., Beck, P. A., Huckfeldt, R., & Koetzle, W. (1998). A test of media-centered agenda-setting: Newspaper content and public interests in a presidential election. *Political Communication, 15*, 463–481.

Danielian, L. (1992). Interest groups in the news. In J. D. Kennamer (Ed.), *Public opinion, the press and public policy* (pp. 63–80). Westport, CT: Praeger.

Dubay, D. (1997, March 20). Evolution, creationism and the N.C. legislature: Is Darwin's theory "true science"? You bet. *The News and Observer*, p. A21.

Gamson, W. A., & Modigliani, A. (1989). Media discourse and public opinion on nuclear power: A constructionist approach. *American Journal of Sociology, 95*, 1–37.

Gamson, W. A., & Wolfsfeld, G. (1993). Movements and media as interacting systems. *Annals of the American Academy of Political and Social Science, 528*, 114–125.

Hansen, A. (1991). The media and the social construction of the environment. *Media, Culture and Society, 13*, 443–458.

Hunter, J. D. (1991). *Culture wars: The struggle to define America.* New York: Basic Books.

Inherit the wind: The state sequel. (1996, March 3). *The Tennessean*, p. 4D.

Kuhn, T. S. (1970). *The structure of scientific revolutions.* Chicago: University of Chicago Press.

Lang, G. E., & Lang, K. (1981). Watergate: An exploration of the agenda-building process. In G. C. Wilhoit & H. de Bock (Eds.), *Mass communication review yearbook* (Vol. 2, pp. 447–468). Beverly Hills, CA: Sage.

Lang, G. E., & Lang, K. (1983). *The battle for public opinion: The president, the press, and the polls during Watergate.* New York: Columbia University Press.

Larson, E. J. (1989). *Trial and error: The American controversy over creation and evolution.* New York: Oxford University Press.

Larson, E. J. (1997). *Summer for the gods: The Scopes trial and America's continuing debate over science and religion.* New York: Basic Books.

Liebler, C. M., & Bendix, J. (1996). Old-growth forests on network news: New sources and the framing of an environmental controversy. *Journalism and Mass Communication Quarterly, 73*, 53–65.

McCombs, M. E., Shaw, D. L., & Weaver, D. (1997). *Communication and democracy: Exploring the intellectual frontiers in agenda-setting theory.* Mahwah, NJ: Lawrence Erlbaum Associates, Inc.

Nelkin, D. (1977). *Science textbook controversies and the politics of equal time.* Cambridge, MA: MIT Press.

Nelkin, D. (1995). *Selling science: How the press covers science and technology*. New York: Freeman.

Neuman, W. R., Just, M. R., & Crigler, A. N. (1992). *Common knowledge: News and the construction of political meaning*. Chicago: University of Chicago Press.

Petersen, J. C., & Markle, G. E. (1989). Controversies in science and technology. In D. E. Chubin & E. W. Chu (Eds.), *Science off the pedestal: Social perspectives on science and technology* (pp. 5–18). Belmont, CA: Wadsworth.

Petty, R. E., & Priester, J. R. (1994). Mass media attitude change: Implications of the elaboration likelihood model of persuasion. In J. Bryant & D. Zillmann (Eds.), *Media effects: Advances in theory and research* (pp. 91–122). Hillsdale, NJ: Lawrence Erlbaum Associates, Inc.

Robinson, C., & Powell, L. A. (1996). The postmodern politics of context definition: Competing reality frames in the Hill–Thomas spectacle. *The Sociological Quarterly, 37*, 279–305.

Spaid, E. L. (1996, March 8). Scopes revisited: South puts creationism into classroom. *Christian Science Monitor*, pp. 1, 5.

Taylor, C. A., & Condit, C. M. (1988). Objectivity and elites: A creation science trial. *Critical Studies in Mass Communication, 5*, 293–312.

Tennessee lawmakers tarnish state image. (1996, February 26). *The Tennessean*, p. 10A.

Tennessee Senate Education Committee. (1996, February 21). *Education: SB 3229* (Cassette Recording No. 1, Recorder: Morrison, Log Page No. 1). Nashville: Tennessee State Library and Archives.

Waddle, R. (1996, March 3). Time for "Religious Left" to come off of the ropes. *The Tennessean*, p. 2D.

Wade, P. (1996, February 16). Religious overtones enter Tenn. legislature. *The Commercial Appeal*, p. 1B.

Walters, T. N., Walters, L. M., & Gray, R. (1996). Agenda building in the 1992 presidential campaign. *Public Relations Review, 22*, 9–25.

Wills, G. (1990). *Under God: Religion and American politics*. New York: Simon & Schuster.

APPENDIX:
FRAMES USED FOR THIS STUDY

1. Monkey bill frame (con): All references to this legislation as "the monkey bill," or to "monkeying around."

2. Right-wing politics frame (con): All references to conservative politics and the political maneuvering behind this legislation (e.g., "it's politically motivated," "it shows the political clout of the religious right," "it was prompted by legislators needing to shore up their conservative credentials," etc.).

3. Morals and values frame (pro): References to the moral issues and religious beliefs that prompted this legislation (e.g., "the issue is morality," "it's about values," and "it's about truth, not religion"). This frame also includes comments that teaching evolution undermines the church or the family, or contributes to moral decline.

4. Protecting children frame (pro): This frame suggests that children are easily influenced and need to be protected from the negative, confusing, or misleading influence of teaching about evolution. Sometimes those using this frame also assert that children should be able to make up their own minds about creationism and evolution.

5. Education frame (con): All comments regarding the bill's potential negative impact on students and academic performance (e.g., on standardized test scores) and on the quality of education, especially higher education.

6. Unconstitutional frame (con): All assertions about the unconstitutionality of the bill, including references to court decisions striking down similar legislation and upholding the separation of church and state.

7. State's image frame (con): All comments that the legislation is drawing negative national and international media attention and will hurt the state's image (e.g., it opens the state to national ridicule, "makes us look like rubes and yokels") and may discourage businesses from investing in the state.

8. Ridicule frame (con): All comments that ridicule the legislation through name-calling or example (e.g., it's junk, foolish, ridiculous, or Neanderthal legislation or "why not ban the law of gravity next?").

9. "It's serious" frame (pro): The bill's sponsors used this frame to assert the seriousness of their efforts and the legislation (e.g., "it's serious legislation" and "it's a simple bill with broad-based support," etc.).

10. Scopes or history frame (mixed): All references to the 1925 Scopes trial, the original monkey law, and the history of the evolution debate in Tennessee.

11. Evolution and science frame (con): Discussion of the theory of evolution, how evolution works, and Charles Darwin's research. Also, the defense of evolution as science (e.g., "evolution is a proven theory" and "scientists agree it's a fact" [scientific ideology of expertise], and "evolution forms the basis for all biology" [science as useful knowledge], etc.).

12. Evolution and creationism frame (mixed): This frame compares or explains these differing worldviews, or discusses the sources of conflict between religion and science. This frame was used by both sides in this debate, as well as by reporters, columnists, and editorial writers for context.

13. "It's confusing" frame (con): All assertions that the bill should not be passed because it is too poorly written, too confusing, too vague, and so on.

14. Theory frame (mixed): The scientific definition of a "theory" versus the common usage of the word. *Theory* was misused for maximum confusion by both sides in this debate.

15. "Not a fact" frame (pro): Includes all assertions by the bill's supporters that evolution is a "just theory, not a fact," and so should not be taught as a fact.

16. Equal time frame (pro): Equates evolution and creationism as theories of life's beginnings, and calls for fair and equal treatment of creationism in the classroom. Also includes assertions that teachers and students should be allowed to discuss all theories of creation, including creationism.

17. Christian rights frame (pro): This frame asserts that Christians have the right to be involved in politics (e.g., "Christian parents have rights too" and "this bill was introduced on behalf of Christians," etc.).

18. Mandate or local control frame (con): All assertions that the bill is a state mandate that would interfere with local control of schools (e.g., "the state shouldn't dictate curriculum" and "this is legislative interference in the teaching process").

19. Radical right frame (con): This frame labels the bill's sponsors as "right-wingers" or the "radical right," and so on.

20. Secular frame (pro): This frame labels the bill's opponents as atheists or secular humanists; it also includes other references to secular humanism or ungodliness.

21. Agriculture and micro–macro evolution frame (con): Asserts that limiting the teaching of evolution could interfere with teaching selective breeding and genetics in agriculture programs at state universities. This frame also includes discussions of microevolution and macroevolution.

22. Overzealous teachers frame (pro): All references by the bill's supporters to "overzealous" teachers who are teaching evolution as fact instead of as a theory.

23. Intimidate teachers frame (con): This frame describes the legislation as an attempt to "intimidate teachers" and prevent them from teaching evolution. It also includes references to how the bill threatens "academic freedom," or how students could use it to retaliate against teachers.

24. Cost frame (con): This frame asserts that the legislation will be too costly because it will require the purchase of expensive new textbooks for the state's public schools.

25. God and Bible frame (mixed): Both sides in this debate asserted their belief in God—some as a reason why they were voting for the evolution bill; some ("I believe in God but …") as they voted against it.

26. Other (mixed): Any frame not previously defined that received more than one but less than five mentions in the 62 articles included in this study.

JOURNAL OF MEDIA AND RELIGION, 2(1), 29–47

"Molympics"? Journalistic Discourse of Mormons in Relation to the 2002 Winter Olympic Games

Chiung Hwang Chen

Department of International Cultural Studies
Brigham Young University–Hawaii

During the 2002 Winter Olympics, many made the argument that attention on Salt Lake City provided an opportunity to reshape the Mormon image. Using discourse analysis of news magazine and newspaper articles, this article assesses whether media portrayals of Mormons shifted during the Olympics. It argues that a model minority discourse used by journalists in past decades to describe Mormons persisted in most fundamental respects. Some details changed, but larger stereotypical images were not challenged.

A reporter from the *French Weekly Express* went to Salt Lake City to cover the 2002 Winter Olympic Games with certain images in mind: Mormons are a cultish, weird people somewhere between the Amish and Moonies. His editor expected the reporter to explore the theocratic nature of the Mormon Church, the blind obedience of church members who wear fake smiles, and of course the lustful Mormon men with three wives on their arms. The editor expected him to write something about Mormons so readers would laugh over how odd Mormons are. The French reporter later confessed that what he saw in Salt Lake City did not measure up to his expectations; he found Mormons more mainstream than many people thought and described Mormons as normal and respectable people (Berkes, 2002).

This story was reported by National Public Radio (NPR) in early February, prior to the opening of the 2002 Winter Olympic Games. The inclusion of this French reporter's experience in NPR's Mormon story raises the question of how Mormons are known in the United States and the world, and suggests that the media become the channel shaping or reinforcing such images. The French reporter seemed to

Requests for reprints should be sent to Chiung Hwang Chen, International Cultural Studies, Brigham Young University–Hawaii, 55–220 Kulanui Street, Laie, HI 96762. E-mail: chenc@byuh.edu change his view on the Mormons. Clarifying myths in reporters' minds is one thing; constructing stories to meet demand is another. Many Mormons regarded the Olympic Games as an opportunity to rework their images—not only those from historical stereotypes, but also those from the recent Olympic-bid bribery scandal. This article assesses whether media images of Mormons changed with the Olympics. Were stories about Mormons written differently than they were before? Were Mormon images altered, reshaped, or reinforced during this international event?

Using coverage of Mormons by one sector of the media during the 2002 Winter Olympic Games as a case study, I examine journalistic discourse about this religious minority in the United States. I look, especially, at how the rhetorical strategies used in news articles construct and reinforce certain images and thus help determine how Americans know the group. To situate this case study, I compare current findings with previously conducted work (Chen & Yorgason, 1999). That work detailed how the media have constructed Mormons as a model minority, similar to its construction of Asian Americans. This article evaluates whether the Olympic coverage of Mormons differs from the coverage of Mormons in other times.

THE MORMON IMAGE AND JOURNALISTIC DISCOURSE

Polygamy and Danites are the two most prominent stereotypes of early Mormonism.[1] After the birth of Mormonism in 1830, the media had portrayed Mormons as either sexual lechers or heartless murderers (Arrington & Haupt, 1968, 1970; Bunker & Bitton, 1983; Lynn, 1981). However, since the 1930s, to borrow Shipps's (2000) memorable phrase, the Mormons have transformed themselves from "satyr to saint." As Mormon lifestyles approached mainstream American lifestyles, Mormons went from facing fierce derision to garnering admiration. In analyzing news coverage of the Mormons, Lythgoe (1968, 1977) and Stathis (1981; Stathis & Lythgoe, 1977) argued that the media generally painted a positive picture of Mormons, although the image sometimes was disrupted by controversial events such as the race issue in the 1960s and 1970s, and the church's stand against the Equal Rights Amendment and the MX missile in the 1980s.

This is the point at which my research on the Mormon image began: The image shifted from strongly negative to generally positive over its history. Yet I realized from my work on media images of Asian Americans that "positive" images deserve

---

[1]The Danite group was organized in the late 1830s to protect Mormons from mob violence in Missouri and to help rid the church of dissenters. It began crossing legal boundaries by the time it dissolved a few years later. The legend of the Danites grew, however, among non-Mormons and was particularly, although fancifully, regarded as Brigham Young's favored means during the third quarter of the 19th century of dispensing his own brand of vigilante justice in Utah.

careful consideration. Even positive stereotypes can marginalize. Wald (1995) argued that the press is not neutral in regard to issues of power. It often benefits established constellations of social and cultural power and privilege, even through seemingly positive images of minority groups. My previous research (Chen & Yorgason, 1999) pointed to the existence of a model minority image of Mormons in the news media from the 1930s to 1990s. News magazines portrayed the Mormon Church as successful in both wealth and membership growth. They reported that Mormonism is becoming a world religion. Yet at the same time, this image possesses an underside. Through its growing power, the church poses a threat to American society. By the same token, journalists represent Mormons themselves as clean-cut, patriotic, law-abiding, and self-sufficient models of a sort for American citizenship; yet Mormons simultaneously come across as unknowable, un-Christian, and un-American Others. I argued that this model minority discourse preserves established structures of power by simultaneously valorizing conservative ideals while warning against the participation of new groups (e.g., the Mormons) within these power structures.

Other recent research on Mormon images, likewise, shows that this "positive" image is not a simple one. Both Givens (1997) and Austin (1998) found that in the world of fiction, Mormon characters are still associated with some of their old stereotypes. Mormons in some popular literature remain mysterious, sexually lustful, and even murderous. However, Givens noted, this stereotype is not exactly what it seems to be. Images of sexual repression and patriotic obedience and loyalty have been added to caricatures of Mormons and sit uneasily beside the older images. The Mormon caricature remains a touchstone against which America defines itself. However, because America now prizes tolerance for diversity over religious and social orthodoxy, Givens argued, the Mormon image has moved, though unevenly, toward representations of social orthodoxy. In other words, the use to which the Mormon image has been put (defining what America should not be) has remained since the late 1800s, but the specific content has shifted considerably. This is a very important argument, although I think that in making it, Givens overstated the extent to which the ideals of liberalism and progressivism have become dominant American norms. The mainstream, I would argue, still upholds many of the conservative values Mormons are seen to represent.

De Pillis (1996) reached a somewhat similar conclusion to Givens (1997): Mormonism's model characteristics since 1950—capitalism, patriotism, conformity, heterosexuality, and Republicanism—have come to stand for a conservative, traditional American culture in the midst of the "culture wars." A particularly important sign of this, he (and Givens) suggested, is the representation of Mormons that emerges in Kushner's (1994) award-winning play, *Angels in America.* According to De Pillis's interpretation, the Mormon story has become well-enough known and Mormons so mainstream that they can represent to Kushner all that is wrong with the American past—Mormons are the antithesis of a tolerant, progressive, and sexually mature society. Stout, Straubhaar, and Newbold's (1999) analysis of media reviews of Kushner's play echoes this point somewhat, but also notes that an overwhelming majority of reviews did not mention Mormonism at all. This may indicate that Mormonism as a symbol of ultra-mainstream Americanism may not yet be widely accepted.

To Shipps (2000), this question of whether Mormonism has joined the mainstream is vital. Her focus is somewhat different, however, as she centered the issue of whether the Church of Jesus Christ of Latter-day Saints (LDS Church) as an institution has joined the mainstream of American religions, rather than whether Mormons themselves are seen as mainstream Americans. She argued that in the 1990s, the media began to treat the LDS Church as a mainstream religion, as one that is no longer an aberration on the American landscape. Shipps may be right in identifying the early stages of a trend toward the media mainstreaming Mormonism (and Shipps has proven herself to be a wonderfully perceptive prognosticator of trends relating to Mormonism). However, as I argue later, this trend is not yet definitive. If the image of Mormonism is beginning to change, media coverage of the 2002 Winter Olympics should reflect new themes. However, I find that it is by no means certain that this mainstreaming trend will continue (if it is, in fact, underway). When analyzing Mormons as Americans, especially, rather than Mormonism as an American religion, the model minority stereotype persists.

METHOD

This study uses newspaper and news magazine articles as the primary source for analysis. For newspapers, I include national newspapers such as the *New York Times, Los Angeles Times, USA Today, Washington Post,* and *Christian Science Monitor.* For news magazines, I incorporate mainstream news magazines, such as *Time, Newsweek, U.S. News & World Report, The Economist,* and others. To get a larger sample of articles, the time period of the study was not limited to the 17-day Olympic Games. Most of the media started reporting on the event well before the Olympics actually opened. The bribery scandal in 1999, for example, was part of the Olympic story. Yet, to be manageable, this study cannot cover every aspect and the history of the 2002 Olympic Games. I thus restrict articles to roughly a 1-year period leading up to and including both the Olympic Games and its aftermath. That is, the time period covered in this study is from January 1, 2001 to February 28, 2002. However, I did include a November 2000 *U.S. News & World Report* article, because it is both a cover story and the most lengthy article about the Mormon Church printed in that periodical in recent years.

I did not include every story about the Winter Olympic Games. The reports on the Games themselves are not the focus of the study; I was mainly interested in "side stories" that center around the Mormon Church. Within this framework, I located 32 newspaper stories and 28 news magazine articles, indicating that the Mormon Church received much media attention during the Olympic Games. The discourse as a whole is my main emphasis, although individual articles are the basic units for analysis. In other words, in analysis I looked more for the construction and development of the discourse as a whole than to critique individual articles.

MINORITY SUCCESS AND POTENTIAL THREAT

In my previous work, I found that increasing Mormon wealth and membership always attracted journalists' attention. Few stories in the past six decades failed to mention the church's success in these areas. Many journalists reported that the combination of Mormon wealth and devoted membership sustained the church's influence, not only in Utah and Western states, but also nationally and even internationally. Such discourse continued in the coverage of Olympic-related Mormon stories. Sheler (2000) of *U.S. News & World Report* asserted that "by almost any measure, the Church of Jesus Christ of Latter-day Saints is one of the world's richest and fastest-growing religious movements" (p. 59; "Latter-day Saints," 2002). Woodward (2001) in *Newsweek* put the Mormon success into numbers, reporting that this "once hated, hunted ... sect" is now "a global church worth an estimated $25 billion and claiming 11 million members" (p. 46; MacQueen, 2002; O'Driscoll, 2002; Rivera, 2002; Weiner, 2001). Wright (2002) in the *New Yorker* focused on the rapid growth of the LDS Church in membership by comparing the group with other Christian faiths:

> During the past thirty years, the number of [LDS Church] adherents in the United States has increased by nearly two hundred and twenty-five per cent, to more than five million. (In the same period, the ranks of Southern Baptists, the other fast-growing major denomination in the country, have swelled forty per cent, to sixteen million.) At the same time, the memberships of older, more mainstream denominations, such as Methodism and Episcopalianism, have sharply declined.
>
> The number of Mormons through out the world may soon equal that of Jews. (p. 40; Sheler, 2000)

Citing sociologist Rodney Stark's statement from the 1980s, Sheler (2000) reported:

> If current trends hold, experts say Latter-day Saints could number 265 million worldwide by 2080, second only to Roman Catholics among Christian bodies. Mormonism ... "stands on the threshold of becoming the first major faith to appear on Earth since the prophet Mohammed rode out of the desert." (p. 60)[2]

---

[2]A *Time* cover story, "Kingdom Come," by van Biema, Gwynne, and Ostling (1997) also cited the same source. In fact, Ostling's subsequent book (Ostling & Ostling, 1999) became one of the most cited works in Mormon Olympic stories.

An *Economist* article updated these statistics, reporting that Stark "now estimates 50m by 2040. If current growth rates continue, the Latter-Day [sic] Saints will be numbered in the hundreds of millions by 2080 and Mormonism will be, you might say, the first new world religion since Islam" ("The Mormons," 2002, p. 25).

Besides the numerical growth, the deep pockets of the LDS Church still fascinate many journalists. Sheler (2000) wrote that although the Mormon Church "keeps a tight lid on its financial records," journalists have tried to puzzle "bits and pieces of information" together over the years to estimate the wealth of the church. Citing Ostling and Ostling's (1999) book, *Mormon America: The Power and the Promise*, Sheler reported that the "Mormon financial empire[s'] ... assets [are] at $25 billion to $30 billion, and annual revenue approaching $6 billion, at least $5.3 billion of which comes from member contributions" (p. 61; Booth, 2002). Wright (2002) described the church in business terms, listing the holdings of the Mormon Church including an insurance company, various media outlets, more than 150 ranches, farms, and orchards, and so on (see also MacQueen, 2002; Sheler, 2000). Citing *Time*'s 1997 cover story, Wright noted that if it were a corporation, the Mormon Church would be placed in the middle of the Fortune 500 list.

What's wrong with describing the success of a religious minority? Van Dijk (1993) suggested that a significant feature of stories about minorities is that, more than most stories, they convey a sense of threat or unsolved problems. Success is profoundly ambiguous in the model minority discourse. Stories about Mormons fit van Dijk's argument. The celebration of minority success can easily slip into signals of threat. Sheler (2000), for example, quoting Yale professor Harold Bloom, used them-versus-us rhetoric as he informed about the growing Mormon population:

> "The nation," wrote *The American Religion* author Bloom, "will not always be only 2 percent Mormons. The Saints outlive the rest of us, have more children than all but a few American groups, and convert on a grand scale, both here and abroad. ... Their future is immense." (p. 65)

Still quoting Bloom, Sheler (2000) reminded his readers that even though

> no one really knows what portion of the liquid wealth in America's portfolios is held by the Latter-day Saints Church, ... Mormon financial and political power is exerted in Washington to a degree far beyond what one would expect from one voter in 50 [the proportion of America that is Mormon]. (p. 61)

At the same time as they express admiration of Mormon success, Givens (1997) argued, such statements "inevitably [slip] into a rhetoric that evokes old stereotypes and anxieties" (p. 156).

Warnings of religious minority power are especially strong when journalists assume that the minority transforms wealth and manpower into political influence. The majority of Olympic-related Mormon stories described the dominance of Mormons in Utah politics as well as their influence on the national level. A *Los Angeles Times* article typified this theme:

> More than 70% of the state's 2.2 million population is Mormon (1.8% of the U.S. population is Mormon). … The state's entire congressional delegation is Mormon, as is the governor and 90% of the state Legislature, all of the state Supreme Court justices and 85% of Utah's mayors and county officials. Even the local television station that will broadcast the Games is owned by the church. (Cart, 2002, p. A34; see also Egan, 2002; Janofsky, 2002; Sappenfield, 2002; "They Never," 2002; Woodward, 2001; Wright, 2002)

The Economist and The Associated Press described the LDS Church as an "800-pound gorilla which doesn't have to do anything to seem threatening" ("The Mormons," 2002, p. 26; "They Never," 2002).

Some journalists conveyed anxiety about Mormons not through reference to the number of LDS politicians, but through suggestion of how these LDS politicians might transform their beliefs into politics. *The Economist,* for example, stated that "Mormonism retains a distinctive view of the state which derives from theology" ("The Mormons," 2002, p. 26). The article used Chris Cannon, a Mormon Congressman, to support this assertion. The belief in human free agency, the article suggests, influences Cannon's political agenda—a "'leave-us-alone' view of the state"; therefore, Cannon naturally becomes "a conservative Republican" who favors a minimal role for the government.

Egan (2002) of *The New York Times* echoed this view, asserting a subtle but deep tie between church and state in Utah:

> "In all the years I was mayor and my 18 years in the Senate, not once did the church call me up and tell me what to do," said [former senator Jake] Garn, a Mormon.
> But non-Mormons say the church hierarchy does not have to be overt because the state's political and business cultures are dominated by Saints. (p. D3)

Ernsberger (2002) of *Newsweek* portrayed a similar image by quoting James E. Shelledy, the editor of the *Salt Lake Tribune:* "We are a quasi theocracy, there's no question about that. The church does not call lawmakers up and dictate to them. They already know what to do" (p. 46; Cart, 2002; MacQueen, 2002; Wright, 2002). T. McCarthy (2002) of *Time* put it this way: "Mormonism is virtually synonymous with Utah, and the conservative religion has shaped the state politically, socially and culturally" (p. 58). Booth (2002) of *The Washington Post*, shared the same view, saying that "there is … really no other place in America where one religion so dominates daily life" (p. A6). Some reporters used rhetoric with special post-September 11 significance in portraying Mormon Utah. Wright mentioned that Mark Twain and Arthur Conan Doyle described the Mormons in terms similar to those the press uses to describe the Taliban today. Booth compared contemporary Mormon faith in Utah "favorably, to Catholicism in Rome and Judaism in Israel, or un-favorably by its critics, to Islamic theocracies in the Middle East" (p. A6). *The Economist* article also claimed that Mormon Congressman Chris Cannon wanted the LDS concept of the state "to influence governmental reforms in places like Afghanistan, Pakistan and Iran" ("The Mormons," 2002, p. 26).

Wright (2002) went back to history to find the root of this "theocratic empire" and found that "it is striking how much of the dream has been achieved" in modern-day Utah (p. 42). *The Economist* argued that historical Mormon communalism is still in effect in the lives of Latter-day Saints. The article points out that the LDS Church is "extraordinarily demanding" on members in tithe and time—evidence of modern Mormon communalism ("The Mormons," 2002; Sheler, 2000). Through communalism, Wright implied, the LDS Church has been able to sway political policies in the United States toward its own agenda. He reported that the Mormon Church effectively mobilized anti-Equal Rights Amendment movements in 1976 and anti-same-sex-marriage movements in California, Hawaii, and Alaska in 2000 (see also Sheler, 2000). In that year, Wright noted, the church threatened to withdraw from the Boy Scouts of America if the organization allowed gay scoutmasters. The way these articles describe Mormon conservatism recalls what Said (1994) called the Western notion of fundamentalism. As a minority group, Mormons are presented as the Other who went against "the moderation, rationality, executive centrality of ... 'Western' ethos" (p. 310). One possible reading of these articles is that Mormons are extremists who do not share Western values of moderation and rationality. Alternatively, some have argued that the media defines its own supposed liberality through its depiction of apparently conservative religion (Gans, 1985; Hoover, 1998).

Because of certain interpretations of Mormon dominance, many journalists pose the question of whether the Olympic Games were Mormon Games, or what they called "Molympics." The majority of the articles detailed the involvement of the church in the Games through money, manpower, infrastructure, and technology (see Cart, 2002; Clark, 2001; Ernsberger, 2002; Kleiner, 2002; MacQueen, 2002; O'Driscoll, 2002; Wright, 2002). The theme of the games—"Light the fire within" —was described as emerging "out of a more self-determined, Oprah-affirmative modern Mormon theology" (Stuever, 2002, p. C2). Stuever of the *Washington Post* thus concluded, "Underneath, the Molympics rang true and warm" (p. C2). Although journalists gave LDS Church leaders and public relations people a chance to dispute this Molympics assertion in their articles, Booth (2002) concluded that because "the church's influence will be felt everywhere ... the presence of the church at the Olympics [is] inescapable" (p. A6). He quoted a Mormon critic: "[Mormons] are going into everything. ... Taking the Mormons out of the Games is like taking the salt out of the lake. It ain't going to happen" (p. A6). Wright thus argued that Mormons have outgrown their share of power in American politics. He asserted that "a disproportionate number of Mormons have been elected to higher office in America; although Mormons account for only 1.8 percent of the country's population, five of the hundred United States senators are Latter-day Saints" (p. 56). The article, citing Bloom, further suggested that Mormon politics might threaten American democracy when American Mormons are so numerous and so wealthy "that governing our democracy becomes impossible without Mormon cooperation" (Wright, 2002, p. 42; "The Mormons," 2002). A *New York Times* article puts it more bluntly by quoting a non-Mormon Utahn: "If Mormons were left to their own devices, they would own the country" (Janofsky & Goodstein, 2002, p. A1). The discourse about Mormon success seems to suggest a formulaic logic: Mormon wealth + rapid Mormon numerical growth + communalism → political power → threat to free society and American democracy. Deep ambiguity resides in the theme that the LDS Church is rich, successful, powerful, and its influence spreading.

MORMONS AS THE OTHER

My previous work on the Mormon image argues that despite a sense that Mormons represent a certain ideal version of America, the model minority discourse abundantly figures Mormons as a not completely assimilable minority. Over the past six decades, journalists' accounts have signaled, in a multitude of ways and through discussion of a variety of events, continuing Mormon "otherness." The discourse had not changed much, although some nuance was added, in Olympic-related Mormon stories.

One result of these articles, as well as in those from past decades, was to set Mormons apart from mainstream American culture. Quoting Mark Twain, a *New York Times* article described "the empire that the Mormons built" as "a land of enchantment and awful mystery." The story continues:

> Less than a week before the start of the Winter Olympics, as Utah opens its doors to the world, Twain's head-scratching over the cryptic nature of the Beehive State still holds. As [Twain] said, no outsider can truly comprehend Utah, a state whose history and modern life are cluttered with contradiction. (Egan 2002, p. D3)

Reporters thus wondered "what lies behind the church's many veils" and predicted that the Olympics are "Mormonism's moment of truth" (Woodward, 2001, p. 51; see also Sheler, 2000) because Mormon culture, beliefs, the church, and its members would be scrutinized not only by the American media but by journalists from all over the world. Sappenfield (2002) of the *Christian Science Monitor*, for example, summed up the situation in this way: because the Mormon Utah "is among the world's most peculiar—a place largely shaped by one faith," thus "the world will come to Salt Lake City, not only to watch and enjoy, but also to judge" (p. 1; Figueroa, 2001; "The Mormons," 2002). Although the mayor of Salt Lake City included information in press kits about the city's vibrant arts and culture, burgeoning high-technology sectors, commitment to public transport, safe streets, and waist-high powder on the ski slopes, journalists saw a "peculiar people" as more newsworthy than other issues (Booth, 2002). As a *Reuters* story put it, the media wanted "color stories" about this religious minority ("Latter-day Saints," 2002). Utah and its residents, through what Mulvey (1989) perhaps ethnocentrically called a male gaze and what Said (1994) called an imperialistic gaze, essentially became an exotic object to be looked at and closely examined.

Not only Mormons and their culture, but also their garments (underwear) were under scrutiny. Rivera (2002), writing for the *Los Angeles Times*, described the designs, styles, materials, and meanings of the garment. Wright (2002) explained the evolution of the Mormon underwear from long design to a "Calvin Klein jumpsuit sort of thing" (p. 49) to short-sleeved, two-piece garments. He cited a strange story about a Wyoming beauty queen kidnapping a Mormon missionary and trying to force him to have sex with her. Wright reported that the young missionary finally got away because "his garments kept him chaste" (p. 49). Stuever (2002) viewed the garment as "unmentionable no longer," and felt it "a very odd thing indeed" that Mormons, resistant to the "boxers or briefs" of American culture, still keep quiet and reverent about their underwear (p. C2). He went around town asking people whether they wear garments and whether they can show him their "unmentionables." It is predictable that even a talkative ex-Mormon the reporter interviewed refused to answer. "'That's a rude question' ... and grew quiet," the reporter quoted his source as replying. The article concluded, "The Mormons welcomed the world, after all, and showed us what they're all about. Showed us almost everything" (Stuever, 2002, p. C2).

Journalists also signaled Mormon otherness by characterizing Mormons as minorities eager to be accepted in American society. Wharton (2001) of the *Los Angeles Times* used history as a trope to trace the Mormon psyche in this regard. He quoted Colonel Patrick Edward Connor on Utah in 1857—"a community of traitors, murderers, fanatics and whores"—and presumed that this was the general image of Americans toward Utah. He then quoted a local Utahn to support the point: "We have a history of feeling unliked" (p. 17). He acknowledged Salt Lake City is now a "thoroughly American city"; indeed only "a few of Connor's old barracks remain" (p. 17). Yet, he argued, in some ways not much has changed. Salt Lake City, in his view, "awaits another onslaught of suspicious outsiders" (p. 17). Because of this, some journalists noted that Utahns (mainly Mormons) are conscious about their media image. Wharton quoted the church-owned *Deseret News* to show such Mormon worry: "We'll be featured, profiled, photographed and dissected by every media outlet in the world" (p. 17). Cart (2002), also of the *Los Angeles Times*, quoted a different part of the *Deseret News*:

> They'll talk about how wholesome we are and point out the irony of our role in the biggest scandal in Olympic history. They'll walk over to [the mall] and buy that old

standby, the "Eat, Drink and Be Merry, for Tomorrow You May Be in Utah" shot glass. (p. A35)

Both reporters quoted this passage from the LDS paper: "At some point they'll mention Donny Osmond. We'll emerge as caricatures of ourselves" (see also Clark, 2001; MacQueen, 2002).

A *New York Times* reporter brought up the same point by quoting University of Utah professor Theresa Martinez after the Games: "[People here] want to be accepted, it goes so deep" (Janofsky, 2002, p. A15). Wharton (2001) argued that because Mormons want to change stereotypes about them so badly, they "have slipped more than $1 million in secret cash and gifts to Olympic dignitaries, which ignited an international sports scandal. Still, for all their hopes, the residents of Salt Lake fear they will not be taken seriously"[3] (p. 17). MacQueen (2002) commented that Mormons "sold their souls to the devil" to win the recognition through the Olympics (pp. 18–19). The degree of Mormons' desire for acceptance, according to these articles, reached almost to the point of the pathologically pathetic. Wharton concluded:

> Salt Lake might be portrayed in only the broadest strokes, in reports on polygamy and the bribery scandal, in quaint features about a downtown where grain silos stand only blocks from the skyscrapers. Residents might come off as decent and wholesome, which, for the most part, they are. They might seem a little odd. Certainly they worry about what the world thinks of them, but in the end, it doesn't really matter. (p. 42)

As a journalist who possessed some authority over his story, Wharton decided what should matter to this religious minority. He suggested that no matter how worried the Mormons are, how hard they try to alter their image, the media's impact through its images is rather marginal compared to the day-to-day self-definitions that people everywhere produce.

Journalists also reminded readers of LDS minority status by emphasizing Mormonism's supposedly un-Christian beliefs. Wright (2002), for instance, devoted pages of his article to detailing the "uniqueness" of Mormon theology. He asserted that "underlying Mormonism's cultivation of middle-class normality and hard-headed pragmatism is a deep core of mysticism" (p. 48). The mysticism he referred to includes Mormon notions of the Godhead, temple work, and speculation on the origin of Mormon scriptures, including the Book of Mormon. (Wright noted that the book is "written in a florid style—Mark Twain called it 'chloroform in print.'") Woodward (2001) pointed out some changes the LDS Church has made in recent years, including advising the media that the term *Mormon Church* is no longer acceptable (see also Sheler, 2001) to make the Church sound more evangelical. However, he argued,

---

[3]Utah's Jell-O consumption and Mormon underwear made the news and headlines in many Olympic-related Mormon stories; this should be evidence of not being taken seriously.

the LDS Church is by no means going mainstream, quoting historian Shipps that "Mormons now want to stress their affinities with traditional Christianity yet high-light their uniqueness" (p. 48). Wright concluded that Mormons think of themselves as Christians, but to other Christian denominations, "Mormonism is essentially an overgrown cult. The Southern Baptists … have called Mormonism 'counterfeit Christianity.' Even the more accommodating Presbyterians have condemned Mormonism as a polytheistic heresy" (p. 50; see also Egan, 2002; "The Mormons," 2002; Woodward, 2001).

According to many journalists, Utah is also a place that does not fit the spirit of the Olympics. Mormons' wholesome characteristics of "charity, integrity, decency, courtesy … clean living … and [being] work-addicted," as Wright (2002, p. 48) put it, were incredibly enough, in the hands of journalists, obstacles for hosting this international event. A *Time* article, for instance, wondered how "this sober city" gets itself ready for the big party and how "Mormonism will mix with the Olympic spirit" (Figueroa, 2001, p. 52). The author recalled the stereotype of people in Utah as "oddballs who party too little and marry too much" (p. 53). Booth (2002) similarly reported that a common conception about Salt Lake City is that it is "a Dullsville populated by teetotaling missionaries" (p. A1). Penner (2002) of *The Los Angeles Times* asserted that Utah in fact still lives up to its image. With particular criteria for how "fun" should be defined, Penner spent a whole article complaining how boring Utah was. To him, Utah was "the heart of dullness" because it is "the land of buttoned-up Mormons" and it serves only "watered-down beer and carrot-topped lime green Jell-O" (p. B5). He cited an independent film, *SLC Punk*, and described the film as featuring a young punk starting a punk-rock scene in Salt Lake City "banging his head against the boredom, the blandness and the bleakness" (p. B5). Penner, arriving in Utah before the Olympics officially started, like the main character in the movie, saw nothing in Salt Lake City and thus counted his time there, "One day down, 20 to go" (p. B5).

To other journalists, the boredom of Utah resided in its presumably conservative, conformist, and nondiverse culture. Lamb (2002) of *The Los Angeles Times* described this Mormondom "as squeaky clean as a Disney production" (p. A27; M. McCarthy, 2002; Wharton, 2001). MacQueen (2002) portrayed conservative Utah by saying that the state's public indecency law is so sweeping it could be used "to prosecute exhibits of Michelangelo's classic nude *David* sculpture or even displays [of] bare-breasted women in *National Geographic* magazine" (p. 18; Booth, 2002). Similarly, Wharton reported that a Utah woman complained that a local Victoria's Secret poster, which was appearing in malls nationwide, was too "lewd and sexual" (p. 18). Her complaint, Wharton reported, made the evening news and the display was removed. Clark (2001) of *USA Today* thus argued that Utah "fosters a conservative and insular atmosphere that is too G-rated to be interesting" (p. 1D). Woodward (2001) reinforced this view, asserting that almost every member of the Mormon hierarchy is "a successful, politically conservative businessman—and white" (p. 51) who, Wright (2002) added, wears identical black suits, white shirts, and dark narrow ties (see also Janofsky & Goodstein, 2002; T. McCarthy, 2002). Janofsky (2002) of *The New York Times* called on the stereotype by informing his readers that Utah is a state known for its "staggering conservatism," "homogeneity," and for being "fiercely Republican" (p. A15; T. McCarthy, 2002). Stack (2002) of *The Los Angeles Times* described Utah this way:

> This is a place where public officials can still light a scandal by uttering a mild curse word, a state notoriously fond of its guns. And despite the Olympic floodlights, plenty of people would prefer to remain unknown, unseen and old-fashioned. (p. A1)

Quoting Olympic historian Mark Dyerson, Ernsberger (2002) thus asserted that "Salt Lake City [is] a 'strange' place that's 'a little bit out of step' with the rest of the country" (p. 46). Similarly, Janofsky, quoting Martinez, suggested that Utah is like "'a dull, awkward child' suddenly energized and polished by the possibilities of life" (p. A15).

Wharton (2001) reinforced the Mormon conformity image by quoting University of Utah professor Dean May: "The community is more highly prized than the individual" (p. 18). Wharton used Gordon Monson, a sports writer and radio talk-show host, to illustrate this stereotype. Monson moved to Salt Lake from Los Angeles 9 years ago. (By this, Monson does not fit the Utah Mormon stereotype; he is a "newcomer" who brings in diversity.) He was, Wharton reported, "excited about living in their Zion but wary of the reputation that 'everyone walks in lock step, everyone acts the same'" (p. 18). Wharton reported that Monson's columns, which are "determined to prick the notion of Salt Lake as a cloistered society," are criticized by Utahns as "controversial for controversy's sake" (p. 18). Although Monson insists that there are "free-thinking Mormons," the article used May's comment that "cultures are really hard to change" (p. 16) to conclude its view on Mormon conformity. Wright (2002) echoed this view by claiming that "submission to authority is an essential part of the [Mormon] religion" (p. 48). These articles presented an essentialized view of Mormons who are unable to think critically, and they promote simplistic stereotypes by fundamentally separating LDS culture from American culture.

In *Orientalism*, Said (1978) argued that the Occident defines itself through defining the Orient, through identifying the Occident as what the Oriental Other is not. Some journalists used Rocky Anderson, the liberal non-Mormon (to be precise, ex-Mormon) mayor of Salt Lake City to show what Mormon Utah is not; what he tried to accomplish is what Mormon Utah is supposedly opposed to. T. McCarthy (2002) of *Time* magazine used Anderson's "new Utah" to argue "your father's land of Mormon" has been transformed. The article called Anderson "one of the most liberal mayors in the country" and the person responsible for "the drive for a new Utah." He detailed the diversity and progress Anderson has brought into "the puritanical, homogenous white-bread community of Deseret" (pp. 58–59; see also Booth, 2002; Figueroa, 2001). To T. McCarthy, everything new, every change that takes place in Utah was good and implies the old (Mormon) Utah is backward and not worth preserving. Stack (2002) put this point more bluntly. In her article, "Rocky's Road to Progress," Stack asserted that Anderson is "a confessed rabble-rouser, the incarnation of everything you think Utah isn't" (p. A1). She quoted Anderson's friend, Christopher Smart, that "'he's not in step with his own culture'" (p. A1). The article described the mayor in a very human way:

> Anderson shares a house on the edge of the University of Utah campus with his son, a college freshman. He drinks beer. He plays electric guitar. He dates. He doesn't exactly speak his mind—he lays it down as edict. He sees himself as a necessary, modernizing force in this old-fashioned wash of Rocky Mountains. And he makes some people awfully uncomfortable.
>
> There are plenty who don't agree. Anderson has been criticized by city and state leaders for lack of decorum, for plowing ahead single-mindedly, for his tireless ambition to change, update, replace. (p. A1)

Quoting a Mormon critic and the mayor himself, Stack found Mormons "aren't interested in anything progressive" and lawmakers are "right-wing, reactionary, mean-spirited" (p. A14). Anderson appeared in this article as a real person, progressive, modern, liberal, and democratic; Mormons are everything that Anderson is not.

Polygamy, along with liquor laws in Utah, were probably the most popular topics in Olympic-related articles. Few journalists failed to mention polygamy in their stories. This is also probably the most salient signal of Mormon otherness. Journalists used two categories of polygamy stories—serious and humorous. Serious polygamy stories either revealed the "underground life" of modern polygamous families or discussed the controversy over whether or not the Utah government, with many high officials being descendents of polygamists, is willing to crack down on the fundamentalists (Barker, 2002; Cart, 2001; Ernsberger, 2002; LeDuff, 2002; T. McCarthy, 2001; Murr, 2001; Wolfson, 2001). Humorous polygamy stories mainly poked fun at the practice. These articles repeated the clever slogans of liquor companies and resorts and asked whether or not Mormons are offended by advertising slogans such as "Why Have Just One," "Take Some Home for the Wives," and "Wife. Wife. Wife. Husband. High-Speed Quads" (Chawkins, 2002; Clark, 2001; M. McCarthy, 2002; Penner, 2002; "Utah's Holy War," 2001).

Although some of these articles informed readers that the LDS Church abolished polygamy more than 100 years ago, they still perpetuated the stereotype by connecting present-day Mormons to an unfathomable past. Bennett and Edelman (1985) suggested that

> recurring and stereotypical narrative accounts in the mass media can elicit powerful responses of belief or disbelief in distant audiences without bringing those audiences

any closer to practical solutions for the problems that occasioned the stories in the first place. (p. 156)

The recurring image of Mormon polygamy in stories about Mormons—especially in forms that point to the aspects that seem most bizarre—shapes readers' knowledge about Mormons. It gives people knowledge about this group, and yet constrains the forms this knowledge takes. Within the framework of these stories, Mormon polygamy thus becomes one of the few elements of Mormonism that is known by other Americans. At the same time, however, because of inordinate focus on aspects that promote wonder, it remains one of the least understood issues in Mormonism. Journalists distanced Utah from the American mainstream by portraying Mormondom as exotic, unknowable, conservative, undiversified, and lacking in American spirit. Mormons remain Others.

THE AMBIGUOUS POSITION

As Campbell (1998) pointed out, media often create a dual, sometimes contradictory, image of minority groups. Images of Mormons as religious minority and Utah majority sat side by side in Olympic-related stories. Although journalists have always noted the dominance of Mormons in Utah, this was the first time journalists gave significant attention to the relationship in Utah between Mormons and people who are not of the faith. Because Mormons are rigidly conservative, according to many news articles, tension has arisen between Mormons and non-Mormons. As a majority, journalists suggested, Mormons seem to be responsible for the problem. O'Driscoll (2002) of USA Today noted that although the LDS Church has received better press in recent years, the relationship between Mormons and other people seems not to have improved. The reporter cited the Salt Lake Tribune, one of the two major newspapers in Utah, describing the situation as an "'unspoken divide' that permeates Utah life" (p. 11D). Egan (2002) asserted that the divide comes from different lifestyles between Mormons and other residents in Utah. He argued that restrictions on alcohol, tobacco, and caffeine among Mormons "have also fostered an insularity that can make outsiders feel left out" (p. D4; Sappenfield, 2002). Sheler (2002) added that non-Mormons often interpret close-knit Mormon communities as exclusionary, especially when doing business with Mormons. Sappenfield approached the issue from a cultural perspective, calling the coexisting situation of Mormons and non-Mormons a "curious mix," pointing out that "an ever-changing roster of new migrants continually tilts against the city's conservative heritage" (p. 11). The Economist cited history as the root of the conflict, attributing problems to the LDS Church's "isolated, marginal and rigid" nature, which the article suggested, limited the rights of non-Mormons. The article questioned whether this faith "can rid itself of the other feeling it elicits, however unfairly: hostility toward what is different" ("The Mormons," 2002, p. 26; Wright, 2002). Non-Mormons were thus portrayed as going to extreme lengths to counteract the extreme LDS conservatism. T. McCarthy (2002) quoted a member of Utah's gay community to the effect that the gay community has become as visible as it has "partly out of need. The [LDS] community here can be so oppressive, it almost creates the need for a thriving gay and lesbian community" (p. 62). Journalists reported that the church recognizes there are problems in the relationship between Mormons and non-Mormons. Many noted that Gordon B. Hinckley, president of the LDS Church, and M. Russell Ballard, one of the Twelve Apostles, have advised Mormons to not be "clannish" and not adopt a holier-than-thou attitude.

The LDS Church and Mormons in these articles again appear to be overly conservative and intolerant toward people with differences. An essentialized view remains the way in which most of the media see this religious minority, although it is in this case positioned as majority in its own land. Outside forces, new immigrants, and those assuming majority American values are characterized as fresh and progressive. The Mormon–non-Mormon conflict was also described in a one-sided manner. As the problem makers, according to these articles, Mormons themselves should also be the problem solvers. This viewpoint finds little room for compromise between both parties.

Journalists employed conventional story forms to portray Mormons. Although the details sometimes differed based on the newsworthy event or issue of the moment, the underlying sense remained the same: Mormons constitute a clannish minority with significant gaps that separate them from "normal" Americans. The media recognize that Utah is a space where Mormons are a majority and others have to adapt to their ways of life. Yet many news stories have difficulty portraying the relationship as anything more complex than a majority that is unable to see the oddness of its own ways and adapt to the normality of non-Mormons. In this sense, Utah serves as a metonym for the larger (and long-utilized) implication that Mormons are a minority that needs watching so that it does not gain too much power—so that some of its ways do not become American ways. Mormonism still emerges as something of a problem in need of a solution, as Campbell (1995) and van Dijk (1991) might have predicted when they suggested that journalistic discourse of minorities focuses inordinately on problems and conflict. The discourse constantly reminds readers how much separates Mormons from the rest of the country.

CONCLUSIONS

The 2002 Winter Olympics were viewed by many in the media, as well as in the Mormon Church, as an opportunity to reshape the image of the Church and its members. When compared against the model minority discourse—through which so many journalistic stories on Mormons have historically been written—I cannot conclude that much changed. Aspects of the model minority discourse remain hegemonic among journalists. Certainly the Olympics allowed journalists to speak of different events and issues relating to Mormonism, but the underlying themes of the model minority discourse remain. The stereotype suggests that Mormon culture is unduly conservative, rigid, and overbearing. Where a focus on the racialized priesthood, on feminism, or on doctrinal purity allowed journalists to make that point in the past, liquor laws served the same function in relation to the Olympics. The discourse implies that the fundamental problem is that normality cannot flourish in Utah. Articles in years past used Mormon academic "dissidents," feminists, and leaders from non-Mormon churches as yardsticks of normality.[4] Olympic articles used Mayor Rocky Anderson. The details of the discourse sometimes change, but the fundamental points persist.

I want to emphasize that these are not poor stories. Within the general confines of journalistic standards of objectivity and fairness, these stories fare quite well. Much that is interesting and important is discussed. Even the Church itself would probably find much to applaud in many of the stories. The ability of the media to "get things right" and to be fair in the process seems to be increasing over time. Yet stereotypes and discourses are stubborn things. The way to break out of these confines is not simply to be more accurate and fair. Rather, challenging discourses and stereotypes requires formulating the questions and problems differently. It requires portraying Mormons as normal, not only in relation to the terrorist threat, but also in relation to non-Mormons.[5] It requires the use of narrative conventions that refuse to signal typical meanings. By these standards, the coverage of Mormons during the Olympic Games remained discouragingly similar to past stories about this group.

REFERENCES

Arrington, L. J., & Haupt, J. (1968). The intolerable Zion: The image of Mormonism in nineteenth century American literature. *Western Humanities Review, 22,* 243–260.

Arrington, L. J., & Haupt, J. (1970). The Missouri and Illinois Mormons in anti-bellum fiction. *Dialogue: A Journal of Mormon Thought, 5*(1), 37–50.

Austin, M. (1998). Troped by the Mormons: The persistence of 19th-century Mormon stereotypes in contemporary detective fiction. *Sunstone, 21,* 51–71.

Barker, O. (2002, February 19). Family sharing Mormon culture. *USA Today,* p. 10D.

---

[4]Such narratives still appear (e.g., see Sheler, 2000; Woodward, 2001; Wright, 2002). Mayor Anderson, however, provides a new nuance through which Olympic-related stories ascribe conservatism to Mormonism.

[5]It should be mentioned that stories that focus on security and concerns over terrorism gave no indication of Mormon abnormality. Presumably (though this is a much more important question than I have space to adequately cover here), the assertion of a more fundamental Other (terrorists) allows Mormons involved in security to be seen as completely normal Americans.

Bennett, W. L., & Edelman, M. (1985). Toward a new political narrative. *Journal of Communication, 35,* 156–171.

Berkes, H. (2002, February 2). *Olympics shine light on Mormons.* National Public Radio, Weekend Edition.

Booth, W. (2002, January 28). An Olympic challenge. *The Washington Post,* pp. A1, A6.

Bunker, G. L., & Bitton, D. (1983). *The Mormon graphic image, 1834–1914.* Salt Lake City: University of Utah Press.

Campbell, C. P. (1995). *Race, myth, and the news.* Thousand Oaks, CA: Sage.

Campbell, C. P. (1998). Beyond employment diversity: Rethinking contemporary racist news representations. In Y. R. Kamalipour & T. Carilli (Eds.), *Cultural diversity and the U.S. media* (pp. 51–64). Albany: State University of New York Press.

Cart, J. (2001, September 9). Utah paying a high price for polygamy. *Los Angeles Times,* pp. A1, A22–A23.

Cart, J. (2002, January 13). Mormons to let the Games reign. *Los Angeles Times,* pp. A1, A34–A35.

Chawkins, S. (2002, February 16). Utah businesses have faith that ads shalt not offend. *Los Angeles Times,* p. A16.

Chen, C. H., & Yorgason, E. (1999). "Those amazing Mormons": The media's construction of Latter-day Saints as a model minority. *Dialogue: A Journal of Mormon Thought, 32*(2), 107–128.

Clark, J. (2001, July 6). The keys to Salt Lake City. *USA Today,* pp. 1D–2D.

De Pillis, M. S. (1996). The emergence of Mormon power since 1945. *Journal of Mormon History, 22*(1), 1–32.

Egan, T. (2002, February 3). Ideas and trends: Holy land. *The New York Times,* p. D3.

Ernsberger, R. (2002, January 4). Mormons and moguls. *Newsweek International.* Retrieved February 4, 2002, from http://www.msnbc.com/news/69485/.asp

Figueroa, A. (2001, September 10). Salt Lake's big jump. *Newsweek,* pp. 52–53.

Gans, H. J. (1985, November–December). Are U.S. journalists dangerously liberal? *Columbia Journalism Review,* 29–33.

Givens, T. L. (1997). *The viper on the hearth: Mormons, myths, and the construction of heresy.* New York: Oxford University Press.

Hoover, S. M. (1998). *Religion in the news: Faith and journalism in American public discourse.* Thousand Oaks, CA: Sage.

Janofsky, M. (2002, February 25). Utah's changes may be as fleeting as Olympic glory. *The New York Times,* p. A15.

Janofsky, M., & Goodstein, L. (2002, January 20). In spotlight of the Olympics, a quieter Mormon mission. *The New York Times,* pp. A1, A23.

Kleiner, C. (2002, January 28). Mormon mission. *Newsweek,* p. 50.

Kushner, T. (1994). *Angels in America: A gay fantasia on national themes.* New York: Theatre Communications Group.

Lamb, D. (2002, February 24). Provo isn't friendly by accident. *Los Angeles Times,* p. A27.

Latter-day Saints excited but wary. (2002, February 3). Reuters.

LeDuff, C. (2002, February 23). A holdout polygamist, 88, defies the Mormons. *The New York Times,* p. A12.

Lynn, K. (1981). Sensational virtue: Nineteenth-century Mormon fiction and American popular taste. *Dialogue: A Journal of Mormon Thought, 15*(3), 100–111.

Lythgoe, D. L. (1968). The changing image of Mormonism. *Dialogue: A Journal of Mormon Thought, 3*(4), 45–58.

Lythgoe, D. L. (1977). Marketing the Mormon image: An interview with Wendell J. Ashton. *Dialogue: A Journal of Mormon Thought, 10*(3), 15–20.

MacQueen K. (2002, February 11). Church and state. *Maclean's,* pp. 16–22.

McCarthy, M. (2002, January 2). Local ads stir up Utah controversy. *USA Today,* p. 7B.

McCarthy, T. (2001, May 14). He makes a village. *Time,* p. 30.

McCarthy, T. (2002, February 11). The drive for a new Utah. *Time*, pp. 58–62.

The Mormons: The church of the West. (2002, February 9). *The Economist*, pp. 25–26.

Mulvey, L. (1989). *Visual and other pleasures*. Bloomington: Indiana University Press.

Murr, A. (2001, June 4). Underground in Utah. *Newsweek*, p. 49.

O'Driscoll, P. (2002, February 19). Mormons take pride in taking part in Olympics. *USA Today*, p. 11D.

Ostling, R. N., & Ostling, J. (1999). *Mormon America: The power and the promise*. New York: HarperCollins.

Penner, M. (2002, February 13). Getting jiggly with it. *Los Angeles Times*, p. B5.

Rivera, J. (2002, February 23). Mormons' temples reflect faith's aura. *Los Angeles Times*, p. B18.

Said, E. (1978). *Orientalism*. New York: Vintage Books.

Said, E. (1994). *Culture and imperialism*. New York: Knopf.

Sappenfield, M. (2002, January 28). Salt Lake's struggle to join world. *The Christian Science Monitor*, pp. 1, 11.

Sheler, J. L. (2000, November 13). The Mormon moment: The Church of Latter-day Saints grows by leaps and bounds. *U.S. News & World Report*, pp. 58–65.

Sheler, J. L. (2001, March 19). Don't call it "Mormon." *U.S. News & World Report*, p. 51.

Shipps, J. (2000). *Sojourner in the promised land: Forty years among the Mormons*. Urbana: University of Illinois Press.

Stack, M. K. (2002, February 23). Rocky's road to progress. *Los Angeles Times*, pp. A1, A14.

Stathis, S. W. (1981). Mormonism and the periodical press: A change is underway. *Dialogue: A Journal of Mormon Thought, 15*(2), 48–73.

Stathis, S. W., & Lythgoe, D. L. (1977). Mormonism in the nineteen-seventies: The popular perception. *Dialogue: A Journal of Mormon Thought, 10*(3), 95–113.

Stout, D. A., Straubhaar, J. D., & Newbold, G. (1999). Through a glass darkly: Mormons as perceived by critics' reviews of Tony Kushner's *Angels in America*. *Dialogue: A Journal of Mormon Thought, 32*(2), 133–157.

Stuever, H. (2002, February 26). Unmentionable no longer. *The Washington Post*, pp. C1–C2.

They never prophesied mogul skiing. (2002, January 26). Associated Press.

Utah's holy war. (2002, October 27). *The Economist*, p. 33.

van Biema, D., Gwynne, S. C., & Ostling, R. N. (1997, August 4). Kingdom come. *Time*, pp. 50–57.

van Dijk, T. A. (1991). *Racism and the press*. London: Routledge.

van Dijk, T. A. (1993). Stories and racism. In D. K. Mumby (Ed.), *Narrative and social control: Critical perspectives* (pp. 121–142). Newbury Park, CA: Sage.

Wald, P. (1995). *Constituting Americans: Cultural anxiety and narrative form*. Durham, NC: Duke University Press.

Weiner, J. (2001, May 8). The Mo-lympics. *Newsweek* Web Exclusive. Retrieved January 10, 2002, from http://www.lexis-nexis.com

Wharton, D. (2001, November 25). Judgment at Salt Lake. *Los Angeles Times Magazine*, pp. 16–18, 20, 42.

Wolfson, H. (2001, June 3). All in the family. *New York Times Magazine*, pp. 28, 30.

Woodward, K. L. (2001, September 10). A Mormon moment. *Newsweek*, pp. 44–51.

Wright, L. (2002, January 21). Lives of the Saints. *The New Yorker*, pp. 40–57.

JOURNAL OF MEDIA AND RELIGION, 2(1), 49–64

Religion and Topoi in the News: An Analysis of the "Unsecular Media" Hypothesis

Rick Clifton Moore

Department of Communication
Boise State University

Silk (1995) proposed in *Unsecular Media* that journalists operate with a limited series of topoi and that these are borrowed from religion. Silk thus claimed when journalists write about religion, they do so in a way that ultimately supports religious values. In this study, I apply topic analysis to recent news coverage of Jesse Jackson's marital infidelity to determine the extent to which the topos of hypocrisy was employed and whether this employment supported or challenged a religious (as opposed to secular) worldview.

Numerous studies have investigated the relation between mass media and religion (e.g., Buddenbaum, 1986; Dart & Allen, 1993; Hart, Turner, & Knupp, 1981; Hynds, 1987; Maus, 1990; Mowery, 1995; Nordin, 1975), often examining the specific issues of bias and secularization. Popular conception is that media negatively portray traditional religious institutions and thus add to a putative detachment many Americans feel toward those institutions (Silk, 1995, p. 38). Partly on the basis of such popular concerns, researchers have, through various means, attempted to determine historic changes in the amount or nature of news coverage of religion.

One relatively recent discussant in these issues is Mark Silk (1995), whose book *Unsecular Media* challenges the findings of many earlier studies. Silk made the claim that the media do not denounce the basic teachings of established religion in America. Instead, he argued, the media honor religion by using its own concepts in the process of covering it.

Silk (1995) worked out this explanation of the media–religion relation using the concept of *topos*, commonplace ideas that circulate in a given culture that can be

---

Requests for reprints should be sent to Rick Clifton Moore, Department of Communication, Boise State University, 1910 University Drive, Boise, ID 83725. E-mail: rmoore@ boisestate.edu

used in argumentation. Using this concept as a crucial tool in analyzing journalistic practice, Silk sought to understand which topoi (the plural form of the singular topos) are most important in covering spiritual aspects of American life. In doing so, he demonstrated that rather than coming to bury the church, the media come—wittingly or not—to praise it.

This article continues investigation along the line of inquiry begun by Silk (1995). If topoi are a useful way of understanding American news coverage of religion, their applicability should continue into present and future coverage. If theoretically sound, topic analysis should help us understand current media reports of religious activities just as much as it has in the past. With this in mind, I propose using Silk's concept of topoi to better understand news coverage of the Reverend Jesse Jackson. Jackson, a longtime religious activist and civil rights crusader, was accused of (and eventually confessed to) having an affair with a staff worker and fathering an illegitimate child with her. Numerous national and local news organizations carried reports of the scandal.

This also bears some similarity to the two examples of religion news to which Silk (1995) gave thorough analysis in his book: the cases of Jim Bakker and Jimmy Swaggart. Both men's reputations were severely tarnished by sex scandals in the 1980s.[1] In describing news coverage of the two preachers, Silk suggested that it is through the topos of hypocrisy that the news media disempowered Bakker and Swaggart, while empowering the church as a whole. Silk claimed that by choosing to view the two men's transgressions through the lens of hypocrisy, the media supported rather than challenged religious tradition. As he stated it, such news coverage does not show that the media are in a tense relation with religion, rather that "tension is far less important than Western religious culture per se in explaining how the American news media cover religion" (p. 54).

In this article, I explore the extent to which the topos of hypocrisy helps understand the way the media have covered the Jesse Jackson case, and the extent to which such coverage might or might not reflect a process of secularization. More specifically, I argue that Silk (1995) failed to recognize the flexibility of topoi; media have the ability to use topoi that could be perceived to be religious in nature in such a way that their religious dimension is vacated. Although only one topos is examined here, its use in this preliminary analysis of the Jackson case does not appear to support the hypothesis that the media are more unsecular than secular.

TOPOI AND COVERAGE OF RELIGION

Silk's (1995) affinity for topoi as a means of understanding the relation between media and religion is in some ways a reflection of a deeper dissatisfaction with tradi-

---

[1]Of course, Bakker's case was more than a sex scandal, as there were also issues of fraud, issues that eventually were cause for his criminal prosecution and conviction. Jackson's sexual scandal has also led to investigative reporting into whether the civil rights leader's books are in order.

tional means of analyzing such. In his chapter titled "The Phantom of Secularism," Silk reviewed the debate on media bias toward religion and felt that the results of numerous studies are contradictory and inconclusive. As one example, he analyzed coverage of two papal visits—one in 1980, the other in 1993—and concluded that the concept of "secular bias" (quotation marks his) does not elucidate the similarities and differences in coverage between the two. Bias, according to Silk, does little to explain why religion coverage in the media is the way it is.

As an alternative, Silk (1995) proposed analyzing the "general conceptions" (p. 50) that reporters use in writing their stories. These general conceptions, or topoi as the Greeks called them, are commonplace notions that can be used over and over again within the political, social, and religious discussions of a culture. These "offer jurors moral principles for rendering judgment" and "provide the focus (indeed, the rationale) for journalistic narratives" (p. 51). In other words, the topoi of a culture are a reflection of its deep-seated beliefs. They "cast light on our own system of values" (p. 51).

Silk (1995) was not naive in assuming that such values never conflict. Often societal consensus is hard to reach, and topoi will be inconsistent. Editorial writing, for example, is a site where topoi are often made explicit (Silk, 1995, p. 51). Moreover, Silk admitted that occasionally cultural changes occur and topoi must follow (p. 52). Along these lines, nowhere did he suggest that secularization of American society is impossible. He simply indicated that he saw little evidence for such, especially when news is examined from a topical framework.

In his examination, Silk (1995) tried to lay out a series of topoi he felt become apparent when we closely inspect the way the news media write about religion. As noted earlier, Silk felt that these general conceptions are the conceptions not of a secular ethos, but a religious one. Where many critics of the media look at television reports, radio actualities, newspaper stories, and magazine features and see a consistent bias against the religious, Silk saw a pattern of reporting that reflects a willingness to consistently frame stories with conceptual categories that are historically religious in nature. Hence, he said of those who produce the stories we call "news":

> Ignorant of religion, even hostile to it, some news professionals may be; but the images of religion that they put on display reflect something other than their personal ignorance or hostility. When the news media set out to represent religion, they do not approach it from the standpoint of the secular confronting the sacred. They are operating with ideas of what religion is and is not, of what it ought and ought not be—with topoi—that derive, to varying degrees, from religious sources. (p. 55)

Thus, Silk (1995) set out in his book to identify some of the basic topoi that are used to cover religion within the American media, and to demonstrate that such topoi are rooted in Western religious practice. Admitting that his list is not exhaustive, he named seven topoi in his book: good works, tolerance, hypocrisy, false prophecy, inclusion, supernatural belief, and declension (Silk, 1995, p. 55).

HYPOCRISY AS TOPOS

As noted earlier, my purpose is to examine one of Silk's (1995) topoi as a means of discussing the thesis of his work as a whole. That topos was chosen on the basis of its applicability to a recent news event that was related to religion.[2] The topos I have chosen for discussion is hypocrisy.

Hypocrisy is, in Silk's (1995) eye, a popular journalistic subject because "pursuing hypocrites can be fun and games" (p. 89). Moreover, given journalism's perception of itself as watchdog, pursuing hypocrites is virtuous as well. Silk even perceived the media's tendency to seek out hypocrites within religious bodies to be a reflection of the journalist having the role of "protector of people's faith" (p. 82).

This is the theme that Silk (1995) saw in news coverage of Bakker and Swaggart. Following the basic thesis of his book as a whole, Silk suggested that the news media had no vendetta for the two preachers on the basis of their religiosity. Rather, the news media used a religious principle, the principle of hypocrisy, to protect the legitimate religious flock (a flock that might be damaged by the two leaders). From this perspective, pointing out the hypocritical actions of Bakker and Swaggart was less a negative action than a positive action.

Hence, within the theme of *Unsecular Media* as a whole, news reporting on Bakker and Swaggart represents not an attack on organized religion, but a means of supporting it. Silk (1995) claimed that these cases, along with earlier news coverage of Henry Ward Beecher (a famous Congregationalist clergyman accused of adultery in the 19th century), and the Hollywood depiction of Elmer Gantry, reflect a willingness for the media to play by rules set up by established religion.[3] Those rules suggest that acts of religion must be sincere; they suggest that religious practice must be real. For Silk, this perspective makes no sense outside of Western religious tradition. As he described it:

> Hypocrisy, it need hardly be added, is not a violation of the law. It is a deeply embedded Western religious concept, taken from a Greek term for play-acting and used in Job, Isaiah, and the Gospels to denote the false pretense of piety and virtue. (p. 86)

From Silk's perspective, hypocrisy is thus a tool that the media use to let religion be religion, and to let the people know what true religion should be. It is the means by

---

[2]The extent to which the Jackson story is "religion-related" is discussed later.

[3]The case of Elmer Gantry is an interesting one worthy of further investigation. Silk (1995) made an effort to distinguish between the literary account (by author Sinclair Lewis) and the "mass media" account (as portrayed in Hollywood cinema). Within this framework, the claim is that the literary account was too strong "for the mass media" (Silk, 1995, p. 81). In this way, Silk seemed to be suggesting that literature is not a mass medium and does not follow the general patterns he laid out in the rest of his book. Nowhere, however, did he discuss what makes a medium a mass medium, and if the "unsecular" nature he described varies from medium to medium. One might infer from his comments, though, that the news media are more "unsecular" than literature is.

which the media walk beside religion and sustain it. The recurring use of topoi such as hypocrisy when the media are called on to describe religious activities is concrete evidence (for Silk, at least) of the way the media and religion are in a complementary, not agonistic, relationship.

BAKKER, SWAGGART, AND JACKSON: DIFFERENCES AND SIMILARITIES

Although Jesse Jackson is in many ways very different from both Jim Bakker and Jimmy Swaggart, his media scandal demonstrates clear similarities with those of the two televangelists. Moreover, the differences Jackson exemplifies from the other two offer a tremendous locus for examining the power and flexibility of the topos of hypocrisy.

At first glance, Jesse Jackson would seem an odd pairing with the duo whose demise Silk (1995) described. Silk mentioned that "neither Swaggart nor the Bakkers [Jim or his wife Tammy Fae] engaged heavily in politics" (p. 87). Jackson, on the other hand, has been deeply involved in politics since the 1960s, even running for president of the United States on two occasions. In addition, politically and socially, the earlier televangelists would easily be labeled conservatives, whereas Jackson is liberal. Finally, Bakker and Swaggart were on the geographical, social, and political fringes of society—for example, choosing to operate their "ministries" from small cities in the South. When describing them in his book, Silk said they are "hardly from the mainstream" (p. 83). Jackson, in contrast, is widely considered an insider in Washington, DC, the nation's capital and seat of power and prestige.

However, there are also strong similarities between Jackson and the earlier victims of scandal coverage, and the similarities are important for this discussion. Like the other religious leaders, Jackson also built a large "parachurch" organization. With Jackson, perhaps, the distance between the organization (namely Rainbow/PUSH) and the church is quite great, but the religious dimension is still evident. For example, the official organization Web page consistently refers to Jackson as "the Reverend Jesse Louis Jackson" (www.rainbowpush.org). News organizations also use Jackson's religious title and sometimes highlight the religious dimension of his political and social work. One of the most recent news stories on the civil rights leader began with the words "For decades Rev. Jesse Jackson has picketed and prayed and negotiated on behalf of bus drivers, coal miners and steelworkers" (Davey, 2001, p. 1).

As noted in this quotation, another similarity can be seen in media visibility. Bakker and Swaggart had for several years before their downfalls developed a keen sense of how to use the media. Silk (1995) suggested that this was a key factor in their downfalls. In his reading of the events, journalists felt that "living by the media, they deserved to perish by the media" (p. 87). Certainly Jackson is as adept if not more adept at developing media exposure. In fact, Jackson's media exposure has most often been in the news media itself, whereas much of Bakker and Swaggart's prominence in the media was due to paying for airtime or developing their own broadcast channels.

Whether this will lead Jackson to "perish by the media" is yet to be seen, but a third similarity lies in the anticipation of such by some bodies. In the earlier case of Jim Bakker, Silk (1995, p. 83) reminded us that it was Jimmy Swaggart who first cele-brated Bakker's negative press, presumably hoping it would lead to his own increase in power—as if they were in a zero-sum game. Then, Marvin Gorman, another evan-gelist, was instrumental in exposing Swaggart. In the end, Silk claimed it was Jerry Falwell who gained long-term benefit from the fall of the other two (p. 87).

Nobody can guess whether Jackson's prestige will suffer significant damage due to news reports about marital infidelity, illegitimate paternity, or inappropriate use of funds. At least one news organization suggested there are those who would like to see him unseated. Belluck (2001a) described it as follows: "Ambitious members of the black clergy have begun suggesting publicly that Mr. Jackson's role as the na-tion's pre-eminent African-American figure is on the wane and that the time is right for a new generation of leadership" (p. A1).

The basis on which Jackson's role would be waning is open for dispute, and dispute has already begun in the media. In the process of that dispute, much is revealed about the nature of hypocrisy as a topos by which the media report news of religion.

METHOD: ANALYZING NEWS COVERAGE OF THE JACKSON SCANDAL

Although Silk (1995) did not give a careful description of his method, his general goal was to understand how topoi are used to frame news stories. In analyzing the topos of hypocrisy, he used the Bakker and Swaggart scandals as his chief cases. During the process of analyzing these cases he cited two newspaper stories, two sto-ries from *Penthouse* magazine, one from *Newsweek*, one from *Editor & Publisher*, and two books on the subject (see Silk, 1995, pp. 89–90).

To investigate the Jackson case, a more systematic method was used. The Jackson scandal first reached the national press on January 17, 2001, when Jackson openly admitted that he had fathered a child out of wedlock. National newspapers first pub-lished the story on January 18. In this study, an online search of four national newspa-pers (*The New York Times, The Washington Post, The Los Angeles Times,* and *The Wall Street Journal*) between January 18 and January 31 was conducted.[4] The keyword

---

[4]Understandably, these four publications do not necessarily demonstrate how "the media" utilize topoi in covering religion. They should, however, give some sense of how national media do. Clearly more studies of how smaller, more localized media cover such issues are in order. Silk (1995) tended to focus on national media in his book, although occasionally relying on accounts from smaller outlets such as the *Charlotte Observer*.

searched was *Jesse Jackson*. As the intent was to understand how newspapers as a medium utilize topoi, both news stories and editorials were analyzed. Letters to the editor and editorials by guests who had never published in a given newspaper were elimi-
nated from the sample.

In the end, 15 stories were subjected to analysis. *The Wall Street Journal* gave little coverage to the incident, publishing only one article. The other three newspapers were nearly equal with regard to the number of stories they wrote on Jackson
during this period.

ANALYSIS: HYPOCRISY AS TOPOS
IN THE JACKSON SCANDAL

On January 18, 2001, certain embarrassing aspects of Jesse Jackson's private life became public knowledge. When a tabloid came to him with evidence of a child he
had fathered with a former colleague, Jackson was forced to reveal details of his life
he had hidden for some time. Jackson, married to Jackie Jackson for 38 years, re-
leased a statement admitting to an affair with Karin Stanford who, at the time of
the newsbreak, was caring for their 20-month-old child in Los Angeles.

The mainstream press began delving into the story immediately after Jackson's
admission. Within 24 hr, *The New York Times, The Washington Post,* and *The Los Angeles Times* all ran stories. All three led their stories with the issue of paternity. The
lead of *The New York Times* stated that Jackson acknowledged "he had fathered a
child out of wedlock." From *The Washington Post* the wording was that "Jackson has
fathered an out-of-wedlock daughter." From *The Los Angeles Times* it was that "he
had fathered a daughter out of wedlock."

Jackson's persona was certainly a factor in the coverage. All three initial stories
(in fact, all of the news stories studied here) used his title "Reverend" in the first
reference to him. *The Los Angeles Times* designated Jackson as a "Baptist preacher,"
whereas the *New York Times* labeled him a "Baptist minister." *The Washington Post*
made no reference to his religious position other than his ecclesiastical title.

Even so, the religious dimension of the story was strong, and hypocrisy was certainly a key feature in framing the story early in the coverage. One article (Tobar &
Slater, 2001) even mentioned "cries of hypocrisy" in the headline. Only four articles used the word *hypocrisy* or an etymological derivative in their copy. However,
numerous journalists used wording that indicated hypocrisy was a key topos. Some
made the connection themselves; others quoted sources that drew the necessary
inferences to bring hypocrisy into the discussion.

Many writers intimated hypocrisy by simply making mention of Jackson's moral
and religious ties. Kurtz (2001b), for example, quoted television commentator Britt
Hume, who stated, "This is Reverend Jackson, whose standing as a spokesman on ra-
cial and moral issues stems at least in part from the collar he figuratively wears." Tom
Oliphant, a well-known editorial cartoonist was also quoted by Kurtz. For Oliphant,

as with Hume, the moral-religious dimension of Jackson's work was a key factor by which his actions were to be judged. He claimed that Jackson's problems were fair game for the media because Jackson "talked to all of us about morality and sin as well as appropriations." Oliphant made the hypocrisy line blatant—with words reminiscent of Silk's (1995) definition of hypocrisy—when he stated, "There's a private life that's at variance with the public one." Finally, although Britt (2001) spoke for herself in her op-ed piece rather than quoting another journalist, she also saw hypocrisy stemming from the moral–religious dimension of Jackson's life: "When you set yourself up as having considerable moral heft, as Jackson has—and when you court attention that assiduously—your missteps are as much fodder for mindless gossip as Helen Hunt's rumored face-lift" (p. B1).

Jackson's spiritual stature (in itself) does not appear to have been the biggest factor in precipitating the hypocrisy topos, however. At least six different voices were brought forward suggesting that Jackson's hypocrisy was not a general hypocrisy of being religious yet not following one's religious code. By far the most resonant accusation of hypocrisy in all of the articles has to do with Jackson's willingness to visibly counsel Bill Clinton during the president's own sex scandal. Saltonstall (2001) mentioned that Stanford gave birth "months after Jackson began counseling Clinton over the Monica Lewinsky scandal" (p. A2). Belluck (2001b) reminded us that Jackson "served as a spiritual adviser to the Clinton family" (p. A21). Kurtz (2001b) was less delicate, stating that the "tawdry tale was boosted by Jackson's audacity in bringing his then-pregnant girlfriend, Karin Stanford, to pose with Bill Clinton while the reverend was counseling the president over the Monica Lewinsky affair" (p. C1). Kurtz then went on to quote two other journalists who used the Lewinsky connection to justify reporting about Jackson: Steve Coz stated, "You've got the spiritual leader for Bill Clinton during the Monica sex scandal embroiled in an affair of his own. ... It's also legitimate from the aspect of Reverend Jackson's preaching about the moral fiber of America" (p. C1). Clarence Page pointed out, "The White House held up Jackson as a model of moral authority to whom Clinton was turning" (p. C1). Finally, Tobar and Slater (2001) tied the Lewinsky angle back to the general connection to religiosity. They reminded readers that the "child was born during the time that Jackson served as 'spiritual advisor' to Clinton" (p. A1). In addition, they explained that this would have an effect on "Jackson's role as a political leader with a religious standing, the sort of speaker who sprinkles biblical references into his oratory" (p. A1).

Worth noting here, however, is that most references to hypocrisy came early in the reporting of the events. On January 20, the focus of the news stories shifted slightly as financial exchanges between Jackson and Stanford became a key issue of investigation. In addition, Jackson made public appearances in which allies demonstrated continued support for the civil rights leader. At this time, four stories appeared (Belluck, 2001c; "Jackson Thanks," 2001; "Jesse Jackson Plans," 2001; "Rainbow Coalition Stands," 2001) that played down the hypocrisy topos, making no juxtaposition of words and deeds. In these stories the deeds are listed in a brief factual manner and no critics of Jackson are summoned forth. In fact, the Reverend Jerry Falwell is cited in one story ("Rainbow Coalition Stands," 2001) and is listed as having "praised Jackson for speaking forthrightly about the affair" (p. A13). In none of these stories was a reference made to the hypocrisy of the advisory role during the Clinton–Lewinsky matter, other than one brief one ("Jesse Jackson Plans," 2001) where it was downplayed significantly. In that story, *The New York Times* reported, "Mr. Jackson said he received a call from former President Bill Clinton, to whose side Mr. Jackson rushed when Mr. Clinton's own extramarital relationship threatened to topple his presidency" (p. 125).

Oddly, after this shift in tone, no more hard news stories occurred in the four dailies for the month of January. Op-ed pieces took their place, with five being published by the end of the month. Within these five essays, various perspectives were provided on Jackson's style and the appropriateness of the moral judgment that had been provided in the media thus far. Within this discussion, the hypocrisy topos became much less certain.

Dyson's (2001) piece can be summarized with his claim that we "need to acknowledge that our leaders will occasionally disappoint themselves and us" (p. A19). Charges of hypocrisy were inappropriate, according to the author: "Because Mr. Jackson has so prominently urged young people to take the high road of personal responsibility, some conclude that his actions reveal hypocrisy" (p. A19). He stated:

> But it is not hypocritical to fail to achieve the moral standards that one believes are correct. Hypocrisy comes when leaders conjure moral standards that they refuse to apply to themselves and when they do not accept the same consequences they imagine for others who offend moral standards. (p. A19)

Dyson thus concluded:

> The obsession with sexual sin has distorted our understanding of the morality of leadership. Our leaders cannot possibly satisfy the demand for purity that some make. And neither should they try. Leaders who are blemish-free often possess a self-satisfaction that stifles genuine leadership. (p. A19)

For Dyson, then, hypocrisy is not the topos of the story because Jackson is not a hypocrite. Jackson is presumed to be willing to live with the consequences of his actions. He is also presumed to apply those same consequences to others. Hypocrisy is not simply a matter of saying one thing and doing another.

Stuever (2001) also reduced the power of the hypocrisy topos, but by other means. In a tongue-in-cheek piece about the nature of the "love child" (borrowing a term from an old tune by Diana Ross and the Supremes), Stuever suggested that the nation was too busy "finger-wagging" at President Bush's inauguration and President Clinton's pardons to devote much energy to Jackson. In addition, from

Stuever's somewhat sarcastic perspective Jackson's actions were not really that hypocritical:

> Men of the cloth still have a way of shocking us with their love children. We think they should have a special clarity on fidelity, and it hurts to learn over and over that they don't. Jesse Jackson goes into this category, though not quite like priests and bishops or televangelists. Maybe because he doesn't lecture people about sex and purity, sticking instead to equality and politics. (p. C1)

Jackson's selection of politics—rather than sexuality—as a moral message thus gives him more sexual freedom than other religious leaders. We learn here that to label public persons hypocrites is more difficult when they do not publicly address an area in which they are weak.

This does not give Jackson a complete pass, however. Writing in *The Wall Street Journal*, Jenkins (2001) suggested that it is Jackson's political and economic statements that should draw the most scrutiny. As in many other articles I have studied, Jenkins played up Jackson's religious affiliation, referring to him as a "civil rights agitator, preacher, and presidential candidate" (p. A23). Most of all, however, he focused on Jackson's ability to make financial gain while preaching "victimology." In fact, Jenkins suggested the sex scandal was leaked to the press by Jackson's own staff because of disgruntlement not over the sexual infidelity, but financial malfeasance. In Jenkins's own words, the staff was "concerned less with fornication than with where the funds came from to set up his ex-mistress" (p. A23).

Smith (2001) echoed this nonchalance toward the sexual dimension of the scandal, offering an analysis from a French perspective. Her thesis was that Americans are very uptight about sexual matters because of our moral debts to religious Puritans. In France, where the Puritan movement had little impact, extramarital affairs and illegitimate children are not scandalous, as they are in the United States. Smith acknowledged that many Americans do not have a penchant for French morality, claiming "many people saw his actions as hypocritical" (p. E1). Even so, she tried to get to the root of those views. With the assistance of quotes from a "sexologist at the City University of New York" she explained to her readers that Americans are more hypocritical than people from other countries are because "we're still laboring under puritanical, Victorian views" (p. E1). Smith thus brushed off Jackson's hypocrisy as a cultural condition, and even offered hope that such matters will be less salient in the future due to "progress over the last 100 years toward maturity in our sexual attitudes" (p. E1).

In the last entry of the month, Kurtz (2001a) revisited media coverage of the Jackson affair. He did so not from the perspective of journalists as he did in his earlier essay (Kurtz, 2001b), but from the perspective of those who are politically involved. His claim was that the trend in coverage of political sex scandals has become quite predictable. When a conservative is victim of the exposé, conservatives blame the liberal press, whereas liberals claim hypocrisy. When a liberal is victim, the right displays disgust at liberal values and the left attempts to demonstrate that private lives have no impact on public policy. Within the media themselves, "most of the commentariat splits along ideological lines in stunningly knee-jerk fashion" (p. C1).

The most striking thing about Kurtz's (2001a) article is that despite the headline, "After Jackson's Fall, a Rush to Judgment," the essay veered quite far from the original subject and became a treatise on media coverage of scandal in general, not Jesse Jackson's infidelity. After concluding that commentary on and reception of the Jackson affair were predictable, Kurtz discussed two recent editing decisions at *The Los Angeles Times* that had nothing to do with Jackson or reporting on hypocrisy. Perhaps Kurtz was communicating that a rush to judgment in the Jackson case is ill advised, so no judgment was possible whatsoever. Certainly the overall message is that any charge of hypocrisy is itself suspect.

DISCUSSION

Evident from this analysis is the salience of the hypocrisy topos in coverage of a particular religion-related news story. The times when hypocrisy seems to have been most integrated into the discussion is when Jackson's moral and religious persona was most directly relevant to the allegations against him.

What is also evident, though, is that the topos of hypocrisy is not the only means of addressing the story at hand and that many in the media prefer other approaches with fewer religious overtones. During the second stage of reporting described earlier, little mention of hypocrisy was given in spite of the fact that such was possible. Jackson is well known for his discussion of economic matters (particularly economic justice) and any financial improprieties that might be uncovered could certainly have been analyzed as examples of saying one thing and doing another.[5]

However, this issue simply shows the multifaceted nature of many news stories and the way the media are able to focus on the issues they choose. Whether media practitioners select on the basis of their own orientations or based on perceptions of audience interest is not certain, but in this instance there are obvious repercussions in terms of the secular or unsecular nature of the media reports.

For example, in the Jackson case the earliest reports consistently framed stories on the issue of paternity, not marital infidelity. This is problematic from the "unsecular media" perspective. As Silk (1995) pointed out, the topos of hypocrisy tends to relate to matters that are moral, not legal. Hypocrisy, Silk said, "is not a violation of the law" (p. 86). Yet adultery, an issue that is largely moral and has few le-

---

[5]News coverage of the Jackson case has extended beyond the time frame marked for this article. In those stories since January 29, 2001, much attention has been given to Jackson's financial dealings. The extent to which these are framed from a topos of hypocrisy is worthy of future investigation.

gal ramifications, received little discussion in the news reports. Paternity, which implies issues of legality (at least in civil law), received much attention. As investigation into financial matters in Jackson's nonprofit organizations is ongoing, only time will tell if the issue that could relate to criminal law registers with reporters. In any case, of the two issues studied here—adultery and paternity—the one that is least likely to be a legal matter (it is thus a moral issue, not simply a violation of the law) gained least attention. If hypocrisy is the dominant topos and charges of hypocrisy are religion based—not law based—we might expect an even greater emphasis on adultery, not paternity.

One might also argue that between these two issues, most Western religions say more about the former (adultery) than the latter (paternity). Whereas proscription of adultery is undeniably one of the Ten Commandments to be honored by Christians and Jews, no direct mention is made in the Decalogue of siring illegitimate children. For Christians, the topic of adultery is included in the Sermon on the Mount, one of the most sacred texts on ethics.[6] For many adherents of traditional Western religious traditions (Judaism, Christianity, and Islam included) sexual purity in itself is an important aspect of religious life.

Yet in the media reports studied here, this is not the crucial link. Although commentators openly expressed reasons for not dwelling on Jackson's original sexual transgressions, such explanations are not necessarily helpful in demonstrating the unsecular nature of the media. Several of those commentators suggested that Jackson's illicit sexual relations were not (in themselves) that important because Jackson spends little time discussing such matters directly. Presumably then, hypocrisy is only applicable for those areas of a person's life on which he or she speaks out publicly. If hypocrisy is saying one thing and doing another, the best way to avoid such is to not say anything. From this perspective, in the earlier cases of Bakker and Swaggart, tortured analysis of their sexual sins was appropriate because both had occasionally spoken out on issues of sexual sin. As a logical sequitur, because Jackson's focus is usually politics, not sexual morality, his extramarital relationship is not (in and of itself) worthy of media attention.[7] Apparently paternity is more of a political issue, and thus fair game.

---

[6]Although the Sermon on the Mount stresses the importance of righteousness (e.g., in matters of adultery), many understand it to also communicate that humans cannot achieve righteousness in their own actions. Thus, the sermon encompasses both the subject of not judging others and the importance of seeking righteousness. A common understanding is that ultimately true righteousness can only come from Jesus Christ's atoning sacrifice.

[7]This assumes that reporters are reasonably aware of the public rhetoric of religious leaders and can make accurate distinctions between the content of various leaders' rhetoric (a questionable assumption). When Stuever (2001) claimed that Jackson does not lecture people about sexuality, he was clearly suggesting that other religious leaders do. One might hesitate to claim that Jackson never makes pronouncements on sexuality. Moreover, certainly Jackson holds particular beliefs about what is right and wrong. Are we to believe that because Jackson never preached on adultery that he takes no moral stance on the issue?

This logic does not appear to reflect the unsecular world that Silk (1995) envisioned. It demonstrates that a topos can be borrowed and twisted in a way that actually defeats its original purpose. French sociologist and theologian Jacques Ellul (1975/1978) demonstrated this in his book *The Betrayal of the West*, when he pointed out that many use accusations of hypocrisy in a way very different from the original Christian use. He wrote:

> When Jesus called the scribes and Pharisees hypocrites, he was challenging them to live up to the principles they proclaimed. At the present time, the same accusation is nothing but an attempt at self-justification, an excuse for abandoning principles. (p. 55)

When news media representatives charged Bakker and Swaggart with hypocrisy, then, they did not necessarily agree with the sexual mores the two televangelists were preaching from the pulpit. According to Ellul's description of modern charges of hypocrisy, it is possible that the reporters completely disagreed with the morality the preachers espoused. However, by bludgeoning Bakker and Swaggart with their own morality, reporters could feel superior and remove people who proposed that morality (all the better if the reporters did disagree with it). That is, if hypocrisy is seen as saying one thing and doing another, there are two solutions when it is encountered. Jesus's solution—as described by Ellul—was to do as one says. However, if hypocrisy is saying one thing and doing another, the other option is to simply to stop saying what you are saying. In this instance, stop making pronouncements about sexuality.

However, if pronouncements about sexuality are indeed part of the religious practice of a people, to ask them to cease and desist is to move them toward secularity. This is quite different from what Silk (1995) envisioned. He saw the media as strengthening religion by protecting the morality of the church. Succinctly, he stated:

> What had happened at PTL, what Jimmy Swaggart had done, was not just a private matter, was not just financial fraud and sexual peccadillo. It was an abuse of the faith of their followers and, by extension, of all believers. At bottom, that is what the topos of religious hypocrisy is all about, and why there was a remarkably united front of media, evangelicals, *Penthouse* readers, and "Nightline" watchers to heap abuse on the hypocrites. (p. 88)

However, this all assumes that Bakker and Swaggart would stop behaving as they did, would stop their engagement in adulterous affairs. Once they did so, presumably, they could return to talking about the evils of adultery. To see this as the goal of "*Penthouse* readers" is dubious at best.

Moreover, the abuse heaped on Bakker and Swaggart was heavy, whereas the abuse heaped on Jesse Jackson was short-lived, if it was heaped at all. Several reporters were wondering about the effect of their reporting from the start. Kurtz (2001b) noticed right away that "there's no immediate feeding frenzy" (p. C1). Tobar and Slater (2001) ended their report with a quote from a Democratic political consultant who said "I would be shocked if two years from know [sic] we don't look and see Jesse Jackson on the radar screen" (p. A16). Jenkins (2001) noted within a week of the breaking news that "the Jackson rehabilitation has been accomplished in an eye-blink" (p. A23). Oddly enough, one article on the Jackson affair made direct reference to Bakker and Swaggart. Sean Hannity, interviewed by Kurtz (2001b), asked, "Will Jesse Jackson get the same treatment that Jimmy Swaggart and Jim Bakker got when they were exposed? Will the media shame him off the public stage?" (p. C1). At this point, the evidence suggests the answer to both questions is negative.

CONCLUSIONS

One possible reason for the difference in coverage of these scandals is that Jackson's religion is much less evident than either Bakker's or Swaggart's. Such an interpretation does not corroborate Silk's (1995) thesis. In addition, such an interpretation is based on limited evidence available here and is worthy of further empirical investigation. As noted earlier, in this instance the topos of hypocrisy was used briefly. Once it was abandoned, much of the writing tended to question the reasonableness of high expectations of sexual fidelity itself. Rather than discussing means by which extramarital affairs can be avoided—no article offered this—the articles focused on whether marital faithfulness is a worthy and realistic expectation.

This in itself raises questions about the secular or unsecular nature of the media. Other general findings do so as well. As discussed earlier, the use of the topos of hypocrisy need not support religious belief. To begin with, the concept of hypocrisy need not be founded on religious principles. Silk (1995) admitted this when he said that the topoi used to report about religion are derived from religious sources "to varying degrees." In the case of the topos of hypocrisy, two simple questions demonstrate this. Might not one atheist charge another atheist with hypocrisy? If so, does use of the topos indicate religious adherence?

Ellul (1975/1978) suggested that the answer to the first question is yes, and the second is no. Charges of hypocrisy can be used by anyone, and the purpose may be the abandoning of principles, not the strengthening thereof. Although no article directly requested that its readers abandon certain moral principles, some suggested our principles (as a culture) are outdated and abandonment might be worthy of consideration. Given the fact that some of those principles are embedded in Western religious traditions, labeling such abandonment as unsecular seems illogical.

This is not to say that those who recommend abandoning those principles are immoral or amoral. What should be noted is that they are simply proposing codes of morality that are very different from those held by many Americans, who perceive their morals to be based on religious—rather than secular—principles.[8] To propose alternatives to these religious-based principles is certainly permissible (perhaps even admirable) in a democracy. The key area of interest for Silk (1995) is whether the media more often align their ideas with those whose morals are perceived to be based on Western religious traditions, or those who perceive themselves to obtain their morals elsewhere. In regards to the topos of hypocrisy, the media seem to be suggesting nonreligious traditions as sources for moral authority just as much (if not more) than religious ones.

Of course, Silk (1995) listed seven topoi that he claimed demonstrate the unsecular nature of the media. I have had time to deal with only one of them. Each of the others is worthy of empirical study. For example, Silk claimed that the media pursue "false prophecy" within religious institutions just as zealously as they do hypocrisy. In doing so, according to Silk, the media lend support to legitimate religious bodies. Is there evidence that the media thus distinguish and honor "true" prophets? Similar questions can be asked of the topos of "good works." As example of this, Silk noted positive coverage of efforts to feed the hungry. However, this might be one good work among many that a religious body performs. For example, some religious groups would think it a good work to prevent abortion by blocking the entrance to a women's clinic. Hence we may ask when Silk claimed that the media honor religion by recognizing its "good works," is there any evidence of activities that religious institutions perceive to be "good works" but are denigrated by the media? Finally, Silk claimed that Western religious institutions are by their very nature "tolerant" and the media are supportive of religion when they expose intolerance in religion. Is his description of most Western religious traditions as "tolerant" accurate? When media expose the intolerance of religious bodies, is the end result greater appreciation for religion as a whole, or simple postmodern relativism toward moral and religious questions?

As with the study just presented, in each of these cases there is a need for thorough investigation of the topos, the accuracy of Silk's (1995) description of it, and the effects of its use in the media. The overriding finding here is that a topos may have some of its roots in a religious tradition and yet be used in a way that calls into question traditional religious practice. Perhaps this insight (if accurate) adds to our understanding of the process Silk encouraged us to contemplate. Silk thus admirably opened up a new avenue for investigating the relation between the media and religion. Other scholars must follow his lead if we hope for deeper insight.

---

[8]Understandably, some who attack morals based on certain religious principles are simply using different interpretations of the same religious tradition to do so. A good example of this is the debate about homosexuality within the Christian church wherein adherents of various positions on the issue all claim to honor Christian scripture (see Batalden Scharen, 2000; Stott, 1998). In the news media accounts here, though, no alternative religious foundations were given. Note how Smith (2001) set up the Puritan tradition within Christianity as a source of moral authority, and contrasts it with an areligious system of morality based on French aristocratic behavior and modern sexology. She gave no basis in Catholic theology for a different view of sexual morality than the "Puritanical" view.

REFERENCES

Batalden Scharen, C. (2000). *Married in the sight of God.* Washington, DC: University Press of America.

Belluck, P. (2001a, March 25). Despite emboldened critics, Jesse Jackson isn't yielding. *The New York Times,* p. A1.

Belluck, P. (2001b, January 19). Jackson says he fathered child in affair with aide. *The New York Times,* p. A21.

Belluck, P. (2001c, January 20). Rainbow Coalition paid $35,000 to woman in Jackson affair. *The New York Times,* p. A9.

Britt, D. (2001, January 19). Another icon falls, and it's not surprising. *The Washington Post,* p. B1.

Buddenbaum, J. M. (1986). An analysis of religion news coverage in three major newspapers. *Journalism Quarterly, 63,* 600–606.

Dart, J., & Allen, J. (1993). *Bridging the gap: Religion and the news media.* Nashville, TN: Freedom Forum First Amendment Center.

Davey, M. (2001, March 21). Unions finance Jackson staffers: Work isn't "quid pro quo," he says. *Chicago Tribune,* p. 1:1.

Dyson, M. E. (2001, January 22). Moral leaders need not be flawless. *The New York Times,* p. A19.

Ellul, J. (1978). *The betrayal of the West* (M. J. O'Connell, Trans.). New York: Seabury. (Original work published 1975)

Hart, R. P., Turner, K. J., & Knupp, R. E. (1981). A rhetorical profile of religious news: *Time,* 1947–1976. *Journal of Communication, 31*(3), 58–68.

Hynds, E. C. (1987). Large daily newspapers have improved coverage of religion. *Journalism Quarterly, 64,* 444–448.

Jackson thanks wife and backers at church. (2001, January 22). *The New York Times,* p. A15.

Jenkins, H. W., Jr. (2001, January 24). Business world: Rainmaker redux. *The Wall Street Journal,* p. A23.

Jesse Jackson plans return to public life. (2001, January 21). *The New York Times,* p. I25.

Kurtz, H. (2001a, January 29). After Jackson's fall, a rush to judgment. *The Washington Post,* p. C1.

Kurtz, H. (2001b, January 19). Tabloid news again floods the mainstream; Jesse Jackson's affair "legitimate story." *The Washington Post,* p. C1.

Maus, M. (1990). Believers as behavers: News coverage of evangelicals by the secular media. In Q. J. Schultze (Ed.), *American evangelicals and the mass media* (pp. 253–273). Grand Rapids, MI: Zondervan.

Mowery, R. L. (1995). God in the New York Times. *The Journal of Communication and Religion, 18,* 85–87.

Nordin, K. D. (1975). *Consensus religion: National newspaper coverage of religious life in America, 1849–1960.* Unpublished doctoral dissertation, University of Michigan.

Rainbow Coalition stands behind Jesse Jackson, urges his return. (2001, January 22). *The Los Angeles Times,* p. A13.

Saltonstall, D. (2001, January 18). Jesse Jackson fathered child with top aide. *The Washington Post,* p. A2.

Silk, M. (1995). *Unsecular media: Making news of religion in America.* Urbana: University of Illinois Press.

Smith, L. (2001, January 26). Perspective; in France, adultery has a certain air of je ne sais quoi; will puritanical, Victorian America ever be continentally blase about cheating? *The Los Angeles Times,* p. E1.

Stott, J. R. (1998). *Same sex partnerships: A Christian perspective.* Grand Rapids, MI: Revell.

Stuever, H. (2001, January 23). The love child connection. *The Washington Post,* p. C1.

Tobar, H., & Slater, E. (2001, January 19). Sadness, cries of hypocrisy greet Jackson's disclosure about child; Scandal: Admission about out-of-wedlock baby will tarnish his political, religious roles, many believe. *The Los Angeles Times,* p. A1.

JOURNAL OF MEDIA AND RELIGION, 2(1), 65–67

BOOK REVIEW

Robyn Sylvan, *Traces of the Spirit: The Religious Dimensions of Popular Music.* New York: New York University Press, 2002. 291 pages. $55.00 cloth. $19.00 paperback.

Reviewed by Daniel A. Stout
Department of Communications
Brigham Young University

Fundamentally, *Traces of the Spirit* is about popular music and spirituality. However, many of its arguments and conclusions are relevant to the broader discussion of religion and media. Robyn Sylvan takes on the complex concept of the "numinous," which has only been marginally explored by media researchers. This is the phenomenon, not easily examined through empirical study, in which people describe experiences with art and music in religious terms. *Traces of the Spirit* deals with the religious factor head-on; it combines interdisciplinary theoretical discussion with ethnographic analysis to push the limits beyond traditional definitions of religion. The book's main premise is that "the musical subculture provides almost everything for its adherents that a traditional religion would" (p. 4). This includes ritual, communal ceremony, worldview, and a sense of community. What results is an ambitious work that makes a cogent argument; the data are both fascinating and compelling. Whether they support sufficiently the author's claims about pop music religion having comparable breadth and depth as that found in long-standing denominations is a question likely to draw mixed reaction.

The book opens with the religious reflections of several young adults. Are they describing traditional religious worship? At first glance, it appears that they are talking about prayer, attending church, or some other religious ritual. However, they are actually discussing popular music events such as Grateful Dead concerts and dance raves. Why does young people's discourse about music contain so many references to the "sacred," "spiritual," and "higher plane?" According to the author, it has to do with the migration from traditional religious locales to other cultural sectors where religion is accessed in ways every bit as meaningful as those in conventional congregations. Yet comparisons between old and new forms are not sufficient for an understanding of religious expression through music; this requires a broader definition of religion. Here's where the numinous comes in. According to the author, pop music is experienced through so many psychological, social, and physiological modes of feeling that it is "one of the most powerful tools for conveying religious meaning known to humankind" (p. 6). This multiplicity of connectors between event and "feeling-response" holds the key to understanding the power of music as a religious experience. Drawing on the work of religion historian Rudolf Otto, Sylvan argues that this distinction in the spiritual realm between the phenomenal (things as they appear) and the numinous (things as they are felt in their essence) is an area deserving of more serious analysis.

In dissecting the numinous dimension of popular music, Sylvan does extensive theoretical, historical, and ethnographic work. Chapter 1 explores seven different levels at which music and religion intersect. Discussion of the "virtual level" is particularly insightful with parallels drawn between the temporal nature of music and "virtual reality." Chapter 2 examines some of the cultural crossroads that give the numinous approach a historical context. It deals mainly with the adaptation of ecstatic West African diasporic religion to Christian modes of worship in both Catholic and Black Protestant churches. Blues, jazz, and rock-and-roll all reveal traces of West African possession religions.

Part II details the author's 1.5-year ethnographic study of the San Francisco music scene. There are separate chapters on Deadheads (Grateful Dead followers), electronic dance raves, metalheads (devotees of heavy metal music), and fans of rap and hip-hop. Fieldwork included attending music events, participant observations, and interviews. Analysis reveals more than casual or off-handed references to religion. Evidence of deeper religious culture than one might expect is found within these groups. Deadheads tie the music experience to actual beliefs about fulfillment and joy; following the band is a type of pilgrimage. The chapter on house, rave, and electronic dance music is an equally fascinating look at the religion–music interface. In these genres, music inspires a religious "trance state" through hypnotic beats and rhythms.

This is not the first work to substantively explore religious experience in the media of popular culture. Beaudoin's (1998) *Virtual Faith: The Irreverent Spiritual Quest of Generation X* touches on a number of similar themes. Hoover's (2001) article, "Religion, Media, and the Cultural Center of Gravity," also elaborates on the cultural shifts from institutionally centered to personally centered religion. Similarly, Hickey's (1997) classic essay, "The Little Church of Perry Mason," argues that narratives in the media are the "churches of everyday life" (p. 142). No doubt, references to these works would have strengthened Sylvan's arguments. However, the unique contribution of *Traces of the Spirit* lies in the richness of the data it presents as well as the historical and theoretical analysis performed on them. The book is likely to be an important stimulus of research questions for years to come. Clear frameworks and units of analysis should guide future research and stimulate interdisciplinary study. For researchers of mass communication, the numinous represents a conceptually rich set of ideas and possibilities that are much needed in the study of media and religion.

One question that the author has not addressed fully concerns the depth of religious communities built around music. Many of these seem like specialized experiences and do not always appear to permeate life in the same way that traditional religious communities do. On the other hand, although such comparisons are important to Sylvan, he has moved past them. Not only is there the issue of how music-related religion compares with traditional forms, but also the question of what these new spiritual expressions tell us about the changing nature of religion itself. If the book stimulates additional research on that subject, it will have made an important contribution.

REFERENCES

Beaudoin, T. (1998). *Virtual faith: The irreverent spiritual quest of Generation X*. San Francisco: Jossey-Bass.

Hickey, D. (1997). The little church of Perry Mason. In *Air guitar: Essays on art and democracy* (pp. 138–145). Los Angeles: Art Issues Press.

Hoover, S. M. (2001). Religion, media, and the cultural center of gravity. In D. A. Stout & J. M. Buddenbaum (Eds.), *Religion and popular culture: Studies on the interaction of worldviews* (pp. 49–60). Ames: Iowa State University Press.

www.ingramcontent.com/pod-product-compliance
Ingram Content Group UK Ltd.
Pitfield, Milton Keynes, MK11 3LW, UK
UKHW020427010325
455677UK00029B/1038